& FEARLESS

How to Go from Being Burned Out,
Unhappy & Unmotivated To Reclaiming
Your Mental Health at Work

NATASHA BOWMAN, JD
The Workplace Doctor

Published by Performance ReNEW Publishing, New York, New York.

Printed in the United States of America.

10 9 8 7 6 5 4 3 2 1

ISBN: 979-8-218-15869-9 (Hardcover)
ISBN: 979-8-218-17892-5 (Paperback)
ISBN: 979-8-218-17961-8 (eBook)

This custom publication is intended to provide accurate information and the opinion of the author in regard to the subject matter covered. This book is memoir. It reflects the author's present recollections of experiences over time. Some names and characteristics have been changed, some events have been compressed, and some dialogue has been recreated. It is sold with the understanding that Performance ReNEW publishing and Natasha Bowman is not engaged in rendering legal, medical, psychiatry, financial, or professional services of any kind. If legal, medical, or other expert assistance is required, the reader is advised to seek the services of a competent professional.

“

This book is dedicated to everyone committed to breaking the stigma of mental illness in the workplace and our communities. I also dedicate this book to my family and friends who have supported me on my journey to cultivating cultures of mental wellness in the workplace and beyond.

If you know someone in
crisis, call the hotline below

Suicide
Prevention Hotline

988

Table of Contents

PREFACE

During the COVID-19 pandemic that began in 2020:
Over 6 million people lost their lives.
Over 9 million workers lost their jobs.
Over 97 000 business owners lost their businesses.

I lost my mind.

No, literally. I morphed from someone who had achieved every professional success imaginable for a Black woman just over forty to someone I didn't recognize.

Was it the global pandemic's uncertainty that threatened to end life as we knew it?
Was it being quarantined in our homes and only being allowed to go outside for limited amounts of time with masks on and to stay six feet away from everyone around us?
Was it because once-thriving businesses were suddenly at a standstill?

For me, it wasn't any of these things. This wasn't even the first time I had lost my mind. I just never had time to notice it went missing before. Before March 202o, my hectic schedule of working a full-time job, and being a successful business owner, professor, author, international speaker, wife, and mother, left me busy. ALL THE TIME. Then, all of a sudden, I was left alone with my thoughts. What I came to understand at that point, with my mind not being preoccupied with my professional endeavors, was that being isolated from my thoughts could be far more dangerous and life-threatening than a brush with COVID-19. I had contracted the virus early and quickly recovered, but, in this case, I faced something that isolation or a vaccine couldn't cure. There were no commercials, Presidential briefings, or Dr. Fauci giving me daily updates on my mental health and advising me about the severity of the disease and how to stay safe. I had no fever, cough, chills, or loss of taste or smell. However, I was convinced that I had lost the most important thing to me—my identity. The person I felt I had been was gone, and I was sure she would never return.

Absent of work, clients, and travel, and in company with only my thoughts, it didn't take me long to realize I had been prone to burying myself in work to mask the peculiar thoughts that often ran through my mind. I knew that working multiple jobs at one time, just for fun, was insane. And writing a viral LinkedIn post on my phone while simultaneously driving through the hectic streets of Manhattan wasn't normal. But I ignored all these warning signs. I stayed out of trouble, was successful, and checked off my goals individually. That's all that counted, right?

Jumping a little ahead to one night while most of the country was still in quarantine during the COVID pandemic when everything came crashing down. I was sitting with a bottle of pills in one hand, and a champagne bottle in the other, while my family slept nearby. The memory of being in an identical mental state twenty years earlier was at the forefront of my mind. That time I checked into a lonely, dark hotel room rented by the hour, downed a bottle of pills, and waited to take my last breath. When the time passed for me to check out and the hotel manager knocked feverishly on my door, I was violently awakened from a deep sleep, vomited all the pills I had taken, checked out of the hotel room, went home, and never told a soul of my suicide attempt. I even went to work the next day as if nothing had happened.

I never thought of that day again until that moment in January 2021, a cold night when I lay in a different cold, dark, lonely room. Twenty years later and doing the same thing: pouring a bottle of pills down my throat and drinking a bottle of champagne. I could barely keep my eyes open; my vision was getting blurry. My breathing slowed. This is it, I thought as I took my final breaths. However, that last minute of my life wasn't playing out in the same way as I had seen depicted in the movies with the happy endings. There were no vivid memories of my wonderful husband, kids, and I running on a beach holding hands and smiling or spending our summers on our boat on Lake Michigan. Instead, I just had one final thought: I'M CRAZY AF.

The truth is my life wasn't flashing before my eyes because I wasn't dying. I have no memories of the next 24 hours after my suicide attempt. I just remember opening my eyes through a hazy vision of strangers removing the strings from my pajama pants and shoes (how did I get shoes on?). I was then escorted to a small room where I was laid on a mattress on the floor, where another stranger watched me eat, sleep, and even use the bathroom. For a moment, I thought I was in prison, but then came I came to realize, I had been involuntarily admitted to a mental health facility. Or the "looney bin," as the old folks used to say back in my childhood.

This wasn't my first time in a mental health facility. In fact, for the previous three years, I had been in one almost daily. My full-time job was as the Chief Human Resources Officer at a mental health hospital. Now, I was a patient at its sister facility. As a hospital administrator, I had actually walked the halls of this hospital, rounding with the staff, and catching glimpses of the patients. And doing my best trying not to stare at them. I mostly wondered about the circumstances in which many of them ended up there. They seemed so "normal," yet they had to be *crazy* for them to be admitted to a psychiatric hospital. Episodically, a patient would elope in search of freedom like a prisoner escaping jail. When I heard the code for an eloped patient announced over the intercom, I secretly hoped they would find their way to freedom. Indeed, something better must be waiting for them on the outside. They weren't criminals, I would think, so what harm could they do to anyone on the outside? "Run, patient, run!" I would cheer quietly.

One day, I witnessed a patient being discharged after being there for many months. He had no family waiting for him at the exit doors with smiles, balloons, and flowers. He wasn't rolled out in a wheelchair by a smiling hospital worker as you typically see when patients are discharged from "regular" hospitals. Instead, the patient was walked to the door with a hospital-issued Metro Card to take the subway or bus anywhere he wanted to go in the city. Every time I walk on the streets of NYC, I look into the eyes of the homeless people lying across the sidewalks, wondering if they may be him.

Now, here I was in a different mental health facility than where I worked after my suicide attempt. During my stay, I was diagnosed with bipolar disorder. I was 42 years old. At first, this came as a complete shock to me. How could I be mentally ill? I'd never harmed anyone. I'd always been good at school and work which was a different perspective than what I had been programmed to believe about people with mental illness. Sure, I had been suicidal before, but did that mean I was…. Sick? Let alone diagnosed with one of the most severe mental health conditions in the books?

Well, yes, that is exactly what it meant.

My perception of mental illness was far different from reality. After my diagnosis, I began researching more about mental health conditions and learned that these can be present in various ways, including being "highly functioning" and undetectable. After further research, things suddenly came into perspective. Since the age of eleven, when I recovered from open heart surgery, I've had this innate ability to bounce back from some of the most challenging situations, life had to offer, juggle multiple jobs simultaneously, and carry a level of confidence that is not usually found in a 5'1 fat, Black woman from Montgomery, Alabama. I had achieved professional success by 40, which many will not achieve in their lifetime. I didn't graduate at the top of my high school class or attend a well-known undergraduate school; my law school was second-tier. Yet, somehow, in corporate America, I had managed to compete with the elite.

I would discover that I had lived most of my adult life in a bipolar *hypomanic* state. My professional ambitions had fueled this manic state. When my career was on pause, everything quickly shifted to a dangerous, uncharted territory that would stick with me for the rest of my life. First, I went into a full-fledged bipolar disorder manic state. During one of the darkest times in global history, I felt on top of the world. My speech was so fast, my husband frequently had to ask me to repeat myself. I also spent an unhealthy time on social media reconnecting with people from high school who turned out to be vultures. They could swindle me out of tens of thousands of dollars and other expensive gifts. That was alarming on its own but not the most startling thing. I was losing interest in my loved ones.

My husband Kent and I had been together for almost twenty years. We weren't just married. We were best friends. He was (and is) the love of my life. He is the husband that everyone has always been envious of. Let's just put it this way, I haven't washed a dish, done laundry, or cooked in a decade. But most importantly, my husband has always been the number one supporter of all my career aspirations. I could go on and on about our love for each other, but one day, during this episode, I woke up from the clear blue sky of my dreams and decided that he was no longer the love of my life. He was, of course, devastated. There were no signs leading to this revelation. There were no fights, arguments, or misunderstandings. The person he woke up to for decades was different, and neither of us knew why. My manic episode resulted in much more dangerous and humiliating things. I'm still too embarrassed to share some of the awful stuff that I engaged in while in mania. But I'll leave it at this: the hurt caused to others was almost irreparable, and I still struggle daily with forgiving myself even though I now know it wasn't "me."

It was the "disease."

My bipolar manic state lasted a few months. Then came the bipolar depressive state. This was triggered after I realized all the harm and hurt, I had caused my immediate family while in mania. Without being diagnosed, I had labeled myself a terrible person who does horrible, unforgivable things. How could I have put my husband through so much hurt and pain without explanation? I couldn't even make anything up to place the blame for my actions on him, or childhood trauma, or anything else. I was crazy AF and didn't feel like I deserved to be on this earth. All these unanswerable questions would swirl around in my head, such as "Why did this happen?" "What if this happens again?" "Will my family ever be able to forgive me for the harm I've caused?" I believed I had no choice but to not stick around and wait and see. The only way I could prevent this from not happening again was for me to take my life.

Fortunately, my suicide attempt was unsuccessful, and now I knew that I was dealing with a mental health condition, so I was beginning to understand and accept my diagnosis more and more.

Then, it suddenly hit me. I didn't know what was on the other side of being diagnosed with a mental illness. I was no longer Natasha Bowman, an accomplished professional known as "The Workplace Doctor." Now I was Natasha Bowman, the psycho with a dark past who had spent time in the "looney bin." I wanted desperately to get past this—to do everything my providers told me was medically necessary to end the cycle between mania and depression. I even had to come to terms with the resolve that I would always function in a "less dangerous" hypo-mania state that I believed had fueled my professional success. Still, even in that state, I would always be one step away from danger. Slowly, I embraced the fact that I would need medication and therapy for the rest of my life as there is no cure for bipolar disorder. I also searched for other people diagnosed with mental health conditions. I read stories of success. Then I read stories of failure. Whatever the outcome was, I felt less and less alone in my journey. I did not know these people, but by them sharing their experiences, they had a more extensive, positive impact on me than I could ever imagine. Could I bring the same hope to others that these people had brought me, I wondered.

Remember that I told you that I worked a full-time job? In addition to that, I also own a workplace consultancy practice built on vulnerability and transparency—particularly on social media.

I've used my platform to discuss encountering racism in the workplace, being a single mother, and even my experience of undergoing open heart surgery in early childhood. I had received thousands of messages that my openness and relatability resonated with so many people.

But would revealing my mental illness have the same impact?

I mean, it took me months and countless hours of therapy and research to "destigmatize" myself. If I had felt such an overwhelming sense of blame and shame, how could I expect my professional community of followers not to do the same? Recently, I've seen a shift in people starting to publicly divulge that they suffer from depression and/or anxiety. At that time, however, people weren't sharing openly their diagnoses of less socially "accepted" disorders such as bipolar disorder and schizophrenia. The only time I saw someone of influence reveal their bipolar disorder diagnosis was after something disastrous had occurred related to their condition. It just so happened that a very public "free Brittney" campaign related to the conservatorship status of pop star Brittney Spears was across the news. Her conservatorship began when she experienced a very public mental health crisis and was allegedly diagnosed with bipolar disorder. The media was filled with images and videos posing Brittney in the most negative light. Crazy even. Again, I was not seeing anything positive emerge from revealing such a condition. But maybe I could change that?

Night after night, I lay in bed contemplating "coming out" about my suicide attempt, inpatient hospitalization, and being diagnosed with bipolar disorder. I weighed the pros, and I weighed the cons. And time after time, the cons outweighed the pros. I had slowly returned to posting on social media after an extended unexplained absence. Still, this burning feeling inside me that my followers deserved an explanation for my absence would not subside. They had earned my vulnerability and transparency. Most importantly, because of the current perspective on the capabilities of people with mental illnesses, I felt an obligation to create a different narrative about mental illness.

Eventually, I decided what I wanted to do. I sat my family down and told them it was time we all shed our blame, shame, and pain and invited others into our mental health journey. Yes, I used the word "our" because the trip was no longer just mine. My mental health crisis had affected my entire family's mental health, and we were all in the process of healing. As such, I did not want to make this journey public without their permission, especially since this revelation to almost 100,000 social media followers would affect us all. My daughter was a teenager, and my son was away at college. Neither of them needed Mama to bring any more uninvited drama into their lives. But, when I shared my plans with them, surprisingly, they all supported my decision without hesitancy.

And so, at 6:30 AM the following day, I posted a professional profile picture of myself to my LinkedIn page with the caption, "THIS IS THE FACE OF BIPOLAR DISORDER," and shared my mental health journey. I then walked away from my phone and laptop to shower and prepare for the day. As I dressed, I could hear my phone buzzing with alerts nonstop—one after the other. Buzz. Buzz. Buzz. I refused to look. Already I had convinced myself there would be a flood of insults and derogatory comments. I had survived a suicide attempt and now faced career suicide, and to be honest, I didn't know which one was worse, as my value as a person continued to be centered on my professional success. Finally, the time came for me to start working, and I had no choice but to look at my phone and laptop. In one hour, my LinkedIn app had accumulated over a thousand notifications! My curiosity got the best of me, so I opened the app and scrolled through the comments. I gasped, covered my mouth, and began to cry. I called out to my husband, "Kent, you've got to see this!" He came over and stood there looking over my shoulder in shock and disbelief.

For the next few days, my phone continued to buzz, alerting me to likes, comments, and direct messages from people worldwide applauding my "bravery" and sharing their own mental health experiences. I read and replied to almost every comment and direct message. I instantly learned that mental illness is an inherent leveler; it doesn't discriminate based on race, age, political party affiliation, economic class, title, or geographic border. Most importantly though, I heard from so many of those who suffer in silence because, as much as they might be willing to work up the nerve to message a stranger like me on LinkedIn, they thought they could never tell their story in public. They feared the shame, blame, and pain that I had experienced, but most notably, they feared the reactions from their jobs. LinkedIn is a professional platform, after all. For most, the fear was palpable. Some didn't expect accommodation; they expected retaliation. Others didn't want to feel humiliated, and I knew all about that.

The post and the response had ignited a movement, and now I had to be ready to be a voice in that movement. Employers and employees alike not only wanted to talk about mental health but, because I had chosen LinkedIn as my platform of choice to share my story, the conversation organically was centered around mental health in the workplace. Discussions about mental health had typically been discouraged in the workplace until recently. As a former c-suite HR executive, I know firsthand how managers have been advised to avoid conversations with employees if they suspected an employee was struggling with their mental health. We've been programmed to believe that as managers, we may say the wrong thing that might land us in legal trouble or, worse, say something harmful. Even as HR professionals, we don't want to deal with these issues head-on. Instead, we, too, would refer an employee to an Employee Assistance Program (EAP) or an internal occupational health office. The driving force behind this avoidance is the stigma that comes with mental illness. Stigma is a mark of disgrace associated with a particular circumstance, quality, or person. The keyword here is "disgrace." Once you have been disgraced in the workplace, unless you have some PR team working tirelessly to restore your reputation, it is difficult to bounce back. That disgrace follows you endlessly, and even when others may have forgotten about it, having endured disgrace continues to lurk in your head indefinitely. I know from experience.

In 2017, I was a rock star as a hospital's Director of Organizational Development. I was quickly promoted within a year of being hired, and even the CEO started to rely on me for advice and guidance, although I wasn't her direct report. At this time, I also began a consulting firm and speaking career as a side hustle and wrote my first book, *You Can't Do That at Work!* As someone with a labor and employment legal background, I wanted this book to highlight the common legal mistakes that I had witnessed managers make in the workplace and ways to prevent them. Unbeknownst to me, a few months after its release, the disgraced movie producer Harvey Weinstein would be publicly exposed for engaging in unthinkable sexual acts, assaults, and harassment in the workplace. These allegations prompted the "Me Too" movement and exposed hundreds of other high-profile people in and out of the film industry. This sent shockwaves through various related organizations and forced them to act. It wasn't that they didn't know that sexual harassment in the workplace was illegal. Now that they were "outed," they had to take steps to deal with the exposed offending players in their workplace.

The first step that many of these organizations took was to adopt the strategies laid out in my book. And just like that, I was headed on a nationally sponsored book tour. The sudden demand and "fame" I received were more overwhelming than I could have imagined. Regarding sexual harassment in the workplace, I felt everyone looked to me for answers. Now I had the stress of working full-time and balancing my newfound success as an author and speaker. Leading into the book tour, I had spent every single vacation day I had available speaking and working on growing my consulting business. I was also trying to keep up with the high level of performance that my employer expected of me. Then, just a couple of weeks before leaving for my book tour, I got a notice in the mail calling me into jury duty the week I was set to depart. I felt the weight of the world on top of my shoulders. I would be gone for nearly three weeks from work. Talk about pressure! I began grappling with whether my book tour would be an ultimate failure by wondering if anyone would even show up. I had the inkling that my boss wasn't too happy with me having this little side hustle of mine that had suddenly become a nationally sought-after service.

The day arrived for me to show up for jury duty. As I pulled up to the courthouse, the palms of my hands began to get clammy. I started to sweat profusely. I let out a cry as if I had just learned of the sudden death of a loved one. After hearing the current state of my distress, I called my husband, and he urged me to return home. I called the courthouse, informed them I was sick and couldn't make it, and headed home. Who I didn't call was my boss. My husband and I scrambled for answers to my current mental state. I had never had a "mental breakdown" before. I thrived in chaos, but today was different. "I need to get away with my thoughts," I exclaimed. My husband had stayed at an upstate New York wellness retreat and recommended I go there. He boasted about the mental clarity that he had enjoyed while there. So, we made a reservation, packed my bags, and I headed off. I still had not called my job to inform them that I had canceled jury duty and was headed to get some help because of my current mental state.

The cell phone service at the retreat was spotty, but the following day, I received a text from my boss asking if I had been selected for jury duty or if I would be returning to work. I grappled with coming up with the words to explain what had happened the day before and where I was. Quite frankly, I didn't think she would believe me. In my head, she would suspect I was heading out early for my book tour. So, I lied, saying, "Yes, I have been selected. I likely will not be back until the end of my book tour." This was a decision I regret to this day.

On the other hand, the wellness retreat was what I needed, and my anxiety started to dissipate. After spending the week there, I headed off to my book tour for the next ten days traveling from New York to Atlanta, Chicago, Houston, and finally, Los Angeles. However, lingering in my mind was the inevitable reality that I hadn't been honest with my boss, and I would have to deal with that when I returned. I arrived back on a Monday and went to the office extremely early to catch up on emails and get my thoughts together on how I would explain my lie and what had happened to my mental health that day. To my surprise, there was another HR leader sitting in my office. I walked in, pretending I didn't know what was about to happen, although my gut had already informed me of the inevitable. But before I could even open my emails, my boss poked her head out from the corner of my door and asked me to come to her office. As I walked in, the other HR manager also came in.

"Would it surprise you that I reached out to the courthouse and was informed that you were not at jury duty the other week?" my boss asked, with the other HR leader sitting there, uncomfortably waiting for my response.

"Yes, it would," I lied again.

She then turned to her computer and read an email from the court clerk confirming that no Natasha Bowman had arrived for jury duty. "Oh!" I exclaimed. "They wouldn't have a record of Natasha Bowman because I was accidentally registered with my maiden name." (That was true.)

She seemed perplexed by my answer, and I saw her ponder over her words and whether she may have been mistaken. She then informed me that I would be suspended while this matter was sorted. I assured her it would be. I just needed to call the courthouse and get it all figured out. I thought the matter was dropped but the next thing I knew, security was escorting me out of the building. Fortunately, this happened so early in the morning that I was spared the shame of my team and colleagues seeing me.

I don't know why I continued to lie. I guess it was easier than telling the truth about my mental state. Either way, it was wrong. I couldn't even reconcile what had happened, let alone explain it to others. Also, was this an indication that my superwoman status was on the line? Was the pressure of being an author and a hospital executive, author, speaker, wife, and mom finally too much for me?

When I arrived home, I received an email that I had been terminated. She had already confirmed with the courthouse that neither of my last names had been on jury duty. Texts started coming in from my team asking me what had happened. One person forwarded me the email she sent out, letting them know I was no longer with the hospital. To make matters worse, it was July 26th. I only had one paycheck left, and my medical insurance was due to expire in four days. I had gone from rock star to rock bottom in just a few hours.

I never returned my team's text messages or calls. I was too embarrassed. I let them believe what they wanted. It was easier that way. I mean, it was true, right? I had lied to my boss. But I was also lying to myself.

Come to find out, that episode in front of the courthouse would not be an isolated incident. I needed to seek medical attention. Spending time at the wellness camp was only a band-aid for a giant gushing wound. I'd already had a previous suicide attempt, and now this. Something just wasn't right. That was for me to figure out and me alone.

Thankfully, being terminated from that job didn't impede me from being hired as the head of HR at the psychiatric hospital, where I was back at being a rock star. I thought I had figured out how to balance my full-time job and my consulting business, while also teaching at three universities, and starting to write another book. Life was great until it wasn't. As I explained earlier, I had been in a cycle of bipolar manic episodes that came with symptoms of high productivity, the ability to go without sleep, and doing things that come with disastrous consequences (such as lying to my employer about being on jury duty). Not to mention bipolar depression. These feelings came with self-pessimism and a sudden loss of interest in the things I cared about (all I felt sitting in front of that courthouse). Looking back, just like my brain was shifting from one polar opposite to another, so were my perceptions of myself at work. I was either a rock star or a disappointment. Whether I felt "regular" or not, I was constantly battling a severe mental health condition.

I am not alone. Before COVID-19, a startling one in five people was diagnosed with a mental health condition. According to WHO, during the first year of the COVID-19 pandemic, the global prevalence of depression and anxiety increased by a massive 25%. Now that the worst part of the pandemic is over, workers across the globe continue to be impacted by its long-term effects. After the height of COVID-19, there was a mass exodus from the workplace as workers refused to return to the same work environments that had been negatively impacting their mental health, which came to be known as "The Great Resignation." The fear of losing the flexibility of remote work has increased anxieties for others who have finally achieved the coveted work-life balance. As I write this book, mass layoffs are occurring in industries that traditionally provided job security and growth. Others are just plain burned out from the treacherous work demands. Despite these growing challenges, organizations are not prepared for the fallout, underscoring the urgent need for a practical framework for employees and employers to be equipped with the tools, resources, and guidance necessary to cultivate cultures of mental wellness.

Over the past years, I've learned that everyone has a mental health journey to share, and many have not received the support they've needed to maintain their mental health at work. As such, they are hesitant to be their own advocates but have allowed me to be their spokesperson for this evolving mental health crisis due to blind spots in the current work environment. I write for the sake of all those who, like me, have spent their entire careers laboring under the weight of this burden without support—either because they were too afraid to speak up or because they were hiding behind a mask that made it easier to ignore the signs that they needed help. But I also write this book for anyone in a leadership role to understand that it is time to enter into these difficult conversations about mental health so that they can help their teams find the freedom to speak the unspoken to equip them with the necessary information for making actionable, genuine change.

The stories of those who have struggled with their mental health have a right to be shared so that workers across the globe can band together to step out of the shadows and demand healthier and more positive work environments. As organizational leaders, it's time to create intentionally inclusive cultures that prioritize holistic human wellness (physical *and* mental) so that every employee can enjoy a place that gives them what they need to flourish. I'm turning my pain into purpose using my workplace expertise, labor, and employment law background, and lived experience working with a mental illness to cultivate cultures of mental wellness for others.

This book is written in four parts that will take you on a journey starting with the unknown and unexplored areas of mental health in the workplace. It will also peel back these complexities so that workers and organizational leaders alike can develop practical solutions. It follows my story and the story of others who have been in places of ambivalence about their mental health to self-discovery of what makes us, collectively, mentally, emotionally, and psychologically safe at work.

Will you join me on this journey?

If so, here it is.

Part I - Crazy & Frightened

Part I of this book is written for you to understand why cultivating cultures of mental wellness are imperative. Countless people are left undiagnosed, untreated, or, on the flip side, are diagnosed with a mental health condition and become frightened about how their mental health status may impact their ability to be valued, respected, and seen as credible contributors to the work environment.

Part II- Crazy & Fighting

Breaking the stigma around mental health conditions is probably one of the most challenging barriers to cultivating cultures of mental wellness. Although increasingly more people are vocal about their struggles with mental health, the lack of empathy and understanding about mental health conditions continues to plague the work environment. Before providing effective solutions for improving mental wellness in the workplace, we must educate ourselves about mental health conditions. We must resolve to remove our biases, fight the stigma of mental illness, create safe spaces for dialogue, and finally invoke the same empathy for mental illnesses as physical illnesses.

Part III - Crazy & Forging Ahead

Part III examines how you and the organizational leaders at your workplace can dismantle the long-standing constructs that have been built, dimension by dimension, stigma, pathologizing, bias, limited resources, inaccessible mental healthcare, outdated laws, and inequitable policies. A strategic framework for addressing these issues will be provided to forge a path for creating healthy and safe workplaces for us and others.

Part IV – Crazy & Fearless

Two years ago, I never imagined being considered one of the top voices for workplace mental health. Or that I would be traveling the globe sharing my journey, and helping organizations cultivate cultures of mental wellness. Today, I'm doing it without hesitation or fear, despite my not always feeling that way. As someone diagnosed with a mental health condition, I know how difficult it can be to ignore the assumptions, biases, and stigma targeted toward you. In this section, I will guide you through fearlessly centering your mental health at work. You will be empowered to be bold and unrelenting in embracing authenticity, rediscovering your purpose and passion, and uncompromising in your pursuit of working in healthy and psychologically safe work environments.

Important Notice!

In full disclosure, I am not a mental health professional. I have not been trained to diagnose or treat mental health disorders. However, due to my work in mental health advocacy, I have the privilege of having mental health professionals in my very close circle and will rely on their expertise. I write not just from the perspective of my lived experience with mental illness but for those who have shared their journeys with me. I write for those who have not yet entered the workplace, for my children and yours, with the hopes that their experience will be different from ours. I dream that they can show their full-authentic selves and our workplaces would be prepared for their authenticity. So that they are not seen for what they can't do but for what they can do, which is anything they put their minds to.

Wait! Before We Get Started:
I'm Bringing CRAZY Back

I know this book's title will make some people uncomfortable and may be controversial for others. *Crazy is a verb, not a noun.* The word **crazy** has often been used to perpetuate a negative stereotype of people with mental illness. The word has also been adopted as a weapon against people with mental illnesses meaning that they are incapable, unstable, and even dangerous to themselves and others. When someone is labeled as crazy, they may get very defensive. But here is why I've chosen to use the CRAZY as part of the title of this book.

When I first started to have abnormal feelings and thoughts as I entered into a bipolar manic episode, I didn't quite know what was going on. My knowledge of mental health conditions was limited. My sister had been diagnosed with bipolar disorder years prior, but because our relationship was strained at that time, I didn't take the time to research exactly what it was (in hindsight, maybe I should have). My son was diagnosed with ADHD about a decade before, but all I was told about the condition was that, with medication, he should be able to focus and behave better at school (which he did). In both of my experiences of living with people with a mental health condition diagnosis, and who often demonstrated unusual behaviors, only one word came to my mind in connection with them: *crazy*. There was just no other way, in my mind, to describe how they were behaving.

My son is one of the most gentle and sweet souls I know, but as he navigated through elementary and middle school, a few days never passed by without us getting a call or letter sent home about his behavior. He wasn't engaging in behavior that would lead to harsh disciplinary action or suspension, but it was little annoying things that were seen as distracting to his teachers in class. For instance, he had difficulties sitting still. Or he was easily distracted. He often spoke out without being called on. He didn't listen. At home, his bedroom was always a wreck. We would spend hours helping him with an assignment only to find it crumbled on his floor the next day. The list went on and on.

I still remember to this day being called up by an expensive preschool that I had enrolled him in at three years old. I was asked to come in for a chat. When I arrived at the classroom, I found his teacher sitting in the hallway by her door with her legs raised and her head tucked between her knees. When she heard my footsteps nearing, she looked up at me with tears and simply said, "I just can't do it anymore." I knew exactly what "it" meant. "It" was my son. The frustration in her eyes said it all. I withdrew him from that school the same day, but it was only the beginning of the frustration felt by teachers, me, and my husband of not knowing why my son did what he did. We took toys away. We gave him extra chores. We did everything and anything imaginable to try to get through to him that his behavior was unacceptable. But nothing worked. Looking back, I can only imagine how he must have felt. He had no intention of disappointing his teachers or us, but he couldn't help himself. "I can't stop myself from doing these things despite the consequences." He must have felt frightened, maybe even CRAZY.

If you look at the definition of the word "crazy," it's complex and broad. According to Dictionary.com[1], the term crazy is synonymous with all those terms that people with mental health conditions don't want to be associated with, such as "mentally deranged," "insane," and "demented." But Merriam-Webster defines crazy as "full of cracks or flaws," "not mentally sound," "impractical," "unusual," "infatuated," "obsessed," and "marked by thought or action that lacks reason." The examples that Merriam-Webster gives are closely aligned with how we typically use the word crazy in our everyday language:
"A taste for *crazy* hats."
"He's *crazy* about the girl."
"The fans went *crazy* when their team won the championship."

When I think about my son, my sister (I'll go into details about her later), and myself during our mental health crisis, our abnormal behaviors were exactly as Merriam-Webster describes. Full of cracks and flaws, impractical, and unusual. For example, when I wanted to abandon my family during my mental health crisis, that was abnormal behavior for me. I'd never had those thoughts before.

When we can't explain something, we often use the term *crazy* to describe it. It's not meant to be used in a derogatory way. It's just language that most people use daily. Here are a couple of other examples that I know I use often:

"Girl, you must be crazy to think I'm going out this late at night!"

---

[1] https://www.dictionary.com/browse/crazy, accessed March 15, 2023.

"My job must think I'm crazy if I'm working on Christmas Eve."

Or think about this. You put your leftovers from dinner in the refrigerator before bed. Around midnight, you wake up for a midnight snack, and your leftovers have magically disappeared from the fridge. You return to bed. You are sure that you put the leftovers in the fridge, but then you start to doubt yourself. "Did I mistakenly throw them away?" "Did I forget the takeout box at the restaurant?" "Did I even go to the restaurant at all?" The following day, you discover the empty leftover container of leftovers in the trashcan, and the moment you comment on it, your child gives you a guilty look. You think, "I knew I wasn't going crazy!" You are not degrading or insulting people with a mental health diagnosis; you have simply resolved a complex issue that worried you all night. "Where are my leftovers? I know I put them in the fridge!"

One of the outcomes of this book is to remove the stigma of mental health conditions and educate and empower people to create safe spaces for dialogue about mental health, seek treatment, and empower support for one another, especially in the workplace. We must start by identifying and understanding how mental health conditions present themselves in ourselves and others. To do that, I think it is essential to use plain everyday language until we are educated on the more inclusive, definitive medical jargon. I am not advocating for you to weaponize the word crazy. Crazy should never be used to describe a *person*. However, crazy can tell *how* someone is acting, feeling, or behaving.

When it comes to uncovering the actual reasons behind the mental health crisis in the workplace and what we must do to conquer this challenge, the path and the conversations that get us there may seem crazy. There is not one part of Merriam's definition of crazy that doesn't align with the current workplace model. Our workplaces are full of "cracks, flaws, and impractical" expectations of our workforces. We are expected to work long hours, and multitask, all while being underpaid, undervalued, and working in toxic work environments.

Merriam also defines the term crazy as: "distracted with desire or excitement," "absurdly fond, and passionately preoccupied." Mmmm, don't those definitions resound with your relationship with work, too?! I am passionately fond and preoccupied with my professional career, as I know many of you are too. I am connected to almost one hundred thousand of you on LinkedIn. I scroll through thousands of posts a day that talk about work. On a platform such as LinkedIn, we frequently promote our achievements and accomplishments, but we also use it to promote the accomplishments and achievements of our organizations (by the way, they love getting those free marketing dollars out of you!). Let's face it, the average person spends one-third of her, his, or their life at work. And that's only if you have one job! For those of us with multiple careers, side hustles, and gigs, we spend even more time dedicated to our careers.

When the COVID-19 pandemic forced us to shift our priorities, most of us soon realized how *distracted and excited* we were to be *absurdly fond* and *passionately preoccupied* with work. Now, we want more or even something different, I should say. We want to work for organizations where we can be excited, fond, and passionate about our work, while not being distracted from other aspects of life that bring us joy and fulfillment. To achieve both, we must be fearless about not tolerating the current expectations and constructs of work. Other words for fearless are bold, courageous, and brave. To be bold, courageous, and brave means that we have to be *fascinated* with being *passionately preoccupied* with dismantling the *cracks and flaws* of the *impractical and unusual* policies, systems, and processes that are causing us to be burned out, unhappy, and unmotivated about reclaiming our mental health at work.

That's why I'm bringing crazy back. The word crazy has a long history of being commonly used, whether in a non-offensive way or to indicate that someone is doing something out of the ordinary. I have decided to use the word crazy as part of the title of this book and reference it throughout because I need what I am trying to convey about mental health conditions to resonate with you. To undue bias, stereotypes, and assumptions, we have to be able to shift perceptions and our current way of thinking. I agree that the word crazy has been associated with harmful and dangerous thinking. It most certainly has. However, I disagree that we should abandon the word altogether from our vocabulary.

If we begin that trend, I can think of a million other words that are sometimes associated with harmful things but can also have different and positive meanings. For instance, when I tell people I've been diagnosed with bipolar disorder, most of the time their initial assumptions are that I am moody, unstable, and perhaps a danger to myself and others. Nothing could be further from the truth. The truth is, bipolar disorder has fueled most of my professional success more so than causing harm. It has allowed me to be highly creative, productive, and confident in my abilities. If I'm honest, I don't know who I would be or if I want to know who I would be without my diagnosis. Just because some people have weaponized bipolar disorder doesn't mean I'll stop referring to my diagnosis when I refer to my condition.

People with a broad range of mental health conditions and who are neurodiverse bring unique gifts and talents to our workplaces each day. It is only harmful when we attach assumptions and stereotypes to our conditions. So, instead of wasting precious time on eliminating certain words from our vocabulary, let's re-examine these words, embrace them, celebrate them, and use them to convey our state of mind where we see fit. So, if you identify with acting *crazy* from time to time, whether that means you're *excited* to be *absurdly fond* and *passionately preoccupied* with work or if sometimes your thoughts are *full of cracks and flaws, impractical and unusual*, that's okay. Be bold with it. Claim it. Being authentic can be frightening and exciting all at the same time.

So, to reclaim our mental health at work—let's get a little crazy.

PART I

Crazy

&

FRIGHTENED

"

Princess Diana was the first person in the Royal Family to discuss her struggles with post-partum depression, bulimia, and self-harm. However, in her typical fashion of wanting to help others, she knew that being transparent about her mental health would benefit others. In being vulnerable about her struggles, she knew she would face stigma. As frightening as it must have been for her to break the cycle of the perception of perfection that the Royal Family always displayed, it was just as important that she be seen as a real person with real struggles. Her vulnerability and transparency would make her one of the most admired people on earth.

CHAPTER 1

REAL PEOPLE. REAL LIVES.

One of my favorite movies is *The Nutty Professor*. Eddie Murphy stars in the movie as the morbidly obese Professor Klump, a brilliant scientist who is kind and has a loving and supportive (and funny) family. However, after drinking a potion he invented for rapid weight loss, a new character, Buddy Love, is revealed as his new persona. Buddy Love is cocky, arrogant, and unkind. But, because Buddy Love is thin, Professor Klump goes to dangerous extremes to keep his persona. But when he realizes that Buddy Love hurts people, he fights to get rid of him and return to his previous bigger, yet kinder self. In the end, he learns that although he could get rid of Buddy Love physically, a part of Buddy Love will always be inside him.

I have tried to explain to others what it's like living with bipolar disorder, and *The Nutty Professor* describes it best. One day, you're living your everyday life, and the next day, you're someone completely different. Someone unrecognizable. You have no control over what this different persona says or does. When in a bipolar manic episode, you frequently want to remain in this euphoric state because all your inhibitions are thrown out the window. You have no conscious holding you back. Rather, you feel like you can accomplish anything, and nothing or no one can stop you. However, once you're out of mania, you just want to return to being your "every day" you. But it's hard to do that. You can't turn episodes on and off on demand. You have no control. And, until you're diagnosed, you have no idea why this is happening to you. It's one of the most frightening experiences you can imagine.

The frightening alarming feeling I described is not just associated with people diagnosed with bipolar disorder but is experienced by many even with other mental health conditions. For those who suffer from depression, one day you may be happy and then the next you can't force yourself to get out of bed. People diagnosed with anxiety disorders may suddenly feel periods of intense fear, discomfort, or a sense of losing control, even when there is no apparent danger or trigger. Or, if you're diagnosed with schizophrenia, you may hear or see things that don't exist. If experiencing these things is already frightening, imagine the fear of suddenly experiencing these uncontrollable symptoms in the workplace.

When I decided to share my bipolar diagnosis with my followers, I hoped my post would encourage others to share their mental health stories. I concluded that the more we "unmasked" ourselves, the more we would be accepted in society and our workplaces. But my vision of igniting a "Me Too" movement of people boldly sharing their mental health journeys was quickly crushed. Don't get me wrong, the post went viral with over 1.3 million impressions and over 25,000 likes and comments. But a different "Me Too" movement was happening in my inbox. The movement was, "I shared my mental health diagnosis with my employer and got fired." The subsequent messages were in essence, "me too." Others experienced a mental health crisis at work and subsequently lost their jobs. One was even jailed and almost lost her career as a lawyer. For those of you who have not been impacted by mental illness, you should know that people living and working with mental health conditions are real people with real lives. We are mothers, fathers, sisters, brothers, executives, caregivers, politicians, homeless, wealthy; you name it, that's who we are. I would say that outside of being human, it's one of the common threads that connect most people regardless of their backgrounds. But unlike many parts of our identities, our illnesses remain invisible. Our attempts to be accepted in society and our workplaces are discarded. Our voices are figuratively silenced. Remaining silent has had a devastating impact. We now move to break our silence, unmask our identities, to invite you into our lives as we share our stories.

Not Guilty! By Reason of Insanity

Tara is an accomplished attorney who has held top legal positions in corporate America. Like many of us in the legal industry, Tara's job caused her to grapple with making decisions that appeared to be in her company's best interest but ethically kept her up at night. Although she was fighting undiagnosed depression and anxiety, she failed to seek treatment due to her fear of being "found out" by her company. So, instead of therapy, she turned to food and alcohol, which resulted in her getting a DUI. Unbeknownst to her, her attorney (who also had several DUIs and has subsequently lost his law license) failed to appear for a court hearing on her behalf, and a bench warrant was issued. She was later arrested when she was pulled over for an expired license plate. She was convicted and lost her law license in one of the states where she was barred. Tara was later diagnosed with bipolar disorder and is now getting treatment for her mental health condition and alcohol abuse. Technically, she is a covered individual under the Americans with Disabilities Act, meaning that employers cannot adversely consider her disability when making employment decisions. However, as of today, her bar license is still suspended, she has a public record of a criminal conviction, and she has been unable to obtain employment. Tara went from being a top legal expert fighting in the justice system to fighting the justice system to maintain her innocence as a credible, capable person. I believe, Tara was not guilty by reason of insanity. It's frightening to think that even attorneys struggle to win these battles. How can someone without that legal background feel like they have a chance?

Beauty and the Beast

In 2019, Cheslie Kryst was crowned Miss U.S.A. Her crowning resonated with me in so many ways. She was a beautiful Black woman who wore her naturally curly hair (like I do), majored in human resources (I'm HR!), and was also a lawyer (me too)! Her smile was infectious, and her intelligence was exceptional. She wasn't just beautiful; she was brains and did us proudly. After Cheslie won the title of Miss U.S.A., I followed her career closely as she became a television correspondent and did pro bono legal work for low-level drug offenders. From the outside, it appeared she had it all and would have a life of incredible accomplishments ahead of her. But, on January 30, 2022, I was heartbroken to hear the news that Cheslie had jumped to her death from a high-rise in New York City, where I lived at the time. The world was shocked. How could someone so beautiful, successful, intelligent, and outgoing not want to continue living? Unfortunately, I knew the answer to that question all too well as I had been there just a year before.

Cheslie's mother, April Simpkins, described Cheslie as suffering from "high-functioning" depression[2]. I was familiar with that term, and this description made her even more relatable. In the weeks leading to my suicide attempt, no one would have guessed that I was losing my desire to live daily. Although high-functioning depression is not acknowledged in academic psychiatry, it is very real and equally serious. Unlike other forms of depression, people with high-functioning depression do not generally demonstrate the typical signs of depression. We continue to work, attend school, and engage with our families and friends. But, inside, there

---

[2] https://en.wikipedia.org/wiki/Cheslie_Kryst, accessed on March 15, 2023.

is an overwhelming sense of loneliness, fear, and inadequacy. Often, you search for reasons for these feelings but come up empty-handed, which fuels your depression. So, for many of us, the answer is just to keep showing up as our best selves. We continue to reach higher and higher for a bar that, in our heads, is continuously raised. We're taking care of our responsibilities, not harming anyone, and are often highly accomplished. For Cheslie, the beast of mental illness outweighed her beauty, intelligence, and wit. The world will never be the same.

How to Lose Your Job in Ten Days

Nicole is a budding HR professional who had worked for her employer for almost one year when she began to embark on extensive renovations on her home. Reluctantly, she hired her brother-in-law to take charge of this project, but as any good family member would do, he ran off with tens of thousands of dollars for the project without completing the work.

As Nicole and her husband moved forward with another contractor, some of their neighbors decided they were unhappy with the ongoing renovations and began to embark on various schemes to stop them. One of the schemes was to create a public website bashing Nicole and her husband. As an HR manager and recruiter, job candidates often Googled Nicole to learn more about her before their initial interview, and guess what the first site to pop up was? The terrible site that her neighbors posted about her. This caused a lot of stress and anxiety for Nicole. She began seeing a therapist and shared what was happening with her employer. Her employer appeared outraged and empathetic, even agreeing that what she was experiencing was unwarranted harassment. They even decided together that she should start going by her maiden name professionally to avoid job candidates from coming across this site. With everything that was happening, the failed home renovations that came with the loss of significant income, and her lousy neighbors that continued to harass her, Nicole and her husband floated the idea of just moving out of the state to make a new start.

She approached her manager in tears about everything that was happening and even shared that she had been abusing alcohol to cope. Nicole then discussed her plans to relocate and work remotely like some other employees. She had already spent much of her time traveling for the company anyway. After this conversation, she asked her manager, "Am I going to get fired for sharing all of this information?" Her manager responded by saying, "Of course not!" She walked away thinking that her employer understood that she was just weighing her options, but she just wanted to let her employer know she was going through a rough time, hoping for support.

Nicole's life continued on a downward spiral. Merely days after having the conversation with her employer, her mother attempted to take her life. She informed her manager of what had happened and that she needs to take intermittent FMLA to care for her mother. Her employer's response? " I think you should look for another job." Nicole had never received any negative feedback about her job performance before being notified that she should be looking for another job. After hearing all of the pretextual reasons why her employer thought she was no longer a good "fit" for the job, she informed them that she would be taking continuous leave rather than intermittent leave to care for her mother. She was taking intermittent leave as a favor to them anyway. She was fired shortly after that while she was on job-protected leave, mere days after her mother attempted suicide.

Later, Nicole found out the decision to terminate her was made the day after her earlier vulnerable conversation with her employer about her troubles. There was no sympathy, empathy, or mercy as she had thought. Her employer chose to blatantly break the law by firing her while she was on a job-protected leave rather than doing what was right, to give her the support and compassion she needed and deserved during a difficult time in their employee's life. Until this day, Nicole is still waiting for justice to be served.

Is This Jail or a Job?

Biljana was a budding twenty-three-year-old licensed mediator in Slovenia, Europe. As the head of her department, she exceeded all her goals and became the envy of the licensed attorneys in her office. But her workplace environment became toxic, not because she wasn't a licensed attorney or because she was a woman working in the legal field, but because she was from Montenegro, not Slovenian.

After Biljana's direct manager began to travel frequently, she was assigned to an interim director who resented her ethnicity. One of the changes Biljana began to notice was that everyone would have coffee together before she reported to the interim director. However, the interim director assigned her to an administrative task in the mornings that prohibited her from enjoying coffee with her colleagues and resulted in her having her coffee alone.

Additionally, when the organization changed physical work locations, Biljana's colleagues were assigned to private offices, and she was placed in a cubicle. The tipping point was when her director returned from traveling. He was told by the interim director that Biljana should be placed on administrative duties and that her fourteen colleagues should observe her as she worked and report to him daily about how she was performing. But the catch was that they weren't reporting on her work performance. Instead, they would observe and report on how often she looked at her phone and how often she went to the bathroom. After hearing this, she found herself crying every morning before going to work. Her husband finally asked her, "Are you going to work or jail?"

After a month of her colleagues watching her every move, the Director called her into his office to read what her colleagues had reported. The feedback was horrific. Her colleagues were watching her more closely than she could have ever imagined. The reports were as detailed as how well she cleaned up after herself. After this traumatizing meeting, she returned home and slept for 72 hours straight. She simply could not get out of bed. Her body completely shut down. She then went on sick leave for six months and began seeing a psychiatrist. However, even medical intervention didn't help her. Eventually, she and her husband decided that she should resign from her job. But after consulting a friend that was a judge, she was told that she shouldn't resign but sue her employer.

Biljana did settle with her company and signed a non-disclosure agreement. After that incident, she stayed home for two years. For the first year, she slept constantly on the couch in the living room. It got so bad that her doctors feared that she would develop agoraphobia. She was hospitalized twice when prescription medications failed to help her with her mental health issues. Although this occurred many years ago, she is still affected by this experience. She was eventually diagnosed with clinical anxiety disorder and borderline personality disorder. These disorders' symptoms were never present before working in such a toxic environment. When she finally returned to the workforce, she also experienced PTSD due to her previous work experience. She could not stay in a job for an extended period because as soon as she recognized any toxicity, she immediately resigned.

However, Biljana was able to make a positive change that lasted for some time by starting her own company as an Airbnb property manager, which made her happy and did not cause her any of the triggers she experienced working for an organization. But unfortunately, that company shuttered during COVID-19. She is still trying to find her place in the professional workforce where she deserves to be safe, healthy, and free of toxicity.

A League of Her Own

It's no secret that to get accepted into an Ivy League institution you must embody an impeccable work ethic, determination, and grit. Well, those attributes are what Kerry personified and after receiving her master's degree from the illustrious Harvard University, she carried those attributes into the workforce. However, unlike the other stories I've shared, Kerry had already been diagnosed with bipolar disorder. Like me and many others with a similar diagnosis, she excelled at a start-up tech company. She was considered a rock star. The company benefitted from the creativity and innovation that was fueled by her bipolar disorder diagnosis.

However, the first two letters in bipolar cannot be ignored. One side of the polar comes with creativity, innovation, and sometimes downright genius, but the disorder also comes with the polar opposite: sadness, loneliness, and depression. After she scaled one department at an inhumane pace, she was quickly promoted to build another. It was then that she stalled.

Day after day, she stared at a blank screen, unable to do anything. To make matters worse, the company was in a frenzy preparing for an IPO (initial public offering). Still, Kerry continued to sink into a dark, lonely hole, unable to complete any task day after day. However, no one seemed to notice that her condition was deteriorating. That is until a new Department Head was hired and said, "I don't know what you do all day." "Nothing," Kerry thought to herself, but the new department head already knew that. She had gone from rockstar to rock bottom. Two weeks later, she was fired.

Kerry soon humiliated herself by asking for loans from family friends to pay her mortgage. When doing so, she received the same lack of empathy from them as she did from her employer. "You have a degree from Harvard. Why are you asking me for money?!" her family and friends would exclaim. With the embarrassment and lack of support from her previous organization, she attempted to take her life. Kerry soon learned that few workplaces are prepared to create spaces for people with mental health conditions like bipolar disorder. Why had her employer not dug deeper about why their former rockstar hit rock bottom? Why didn't they offer her support and resources so she could get back to being the top-performing employee she once was? Why had she been discarded with no empathy and compassion? Until these questions can be answered and resolved,

Kerry decided to take her Ivy League degree to create a league of her own by starting an organization that advocates for mental health.

*****

These stories are just a drop in the number of stories people have shared with me about their experiences of how their workplaces have triggered mental health conditions or exacerbated existing ones. When I reflect on these stories and others, I cannot help but notice a common theme: their employers' lack of compassion and empathy. It's easier for employers to discard people like us rather than look at us head-on and learn more about our situation, how we can be supported, and how to respect us.

Other illnesses in the workplace evoke the compassion and empathy that we need. As Kerry so well stated,

"Perhaps it would be better if I had brain cancer instead of an invisible brain disorder and was undergoing chemo treatment. Yes, my productivity would have been severely impaired, but I would have been offered empathy and grace as my physical disability would have been visible to the naked eye. But, in my case, my depression was not. That is not to say, however, that I did not suffer."

Until organizations finally pull back the curtain on how their environments are significantly contributing to the mental health crisis, there will continue to be millions of people around the world who struggle with existing mental health conditions or who will develop mental health conditions, leaving a story that ends similar to the stories I've shared in this chapter—and will continue to share with you throughout this book. Until then, those with mental health conditions will continue to exist unacknowledged, silenced, and broken. One of the scariest things that can happen during your adult life is not knowing where your next meal will come from, how you'll pay your mortgage, or, even more frightening, not wanting to live another day on this earth due to a condition that has no cure, is life-threatening, and seems to be invisible to the world around you.

For those of us who have not lost the fight despite having an unforgiving and uncompassionate workplace, we will continue to forge ahead, crazy and frightened, wondering when the day will come when we will be discarded. This type of uncertainty can become the master of dark thoughts and it will take the collective whole of humanity to raise awareness, find solutions, and eradicate the desire to fire the problem over the need to inspire the solution.

CHAPTER 2

A QUIET PLACE

In 2018, a movie called *The Quiet Place* was released. In this movie, a family is forced to remain quiet or be killed in a "post-apocalyptic world inhabited by blind monsters with an acute sense of hearing." The plot unfolds as the family fights for survival while remaining silent. While watching this movie with my daughter, she turned to me and said, "You would never survive in a situation where you have to be quiet!" We both laughed, and I nodded in agreement. I like to run my mouth, especially regarding anything work-related. My daughter was right. I would never survive in a quiet place.

Upon reflection on this movie (can you tell I love movies?), both the original and the sequel, I have to disagree with my daughter's and my conclusion that I couldn't remain silent. In reality, I had remained silent more times than I can count in my career. Additionally, I couldn't help but equate the challenges the characters were going through with those that are suffered by people with mental health disorders in the workplace. It can feel like if someone at work finds out you're "crazy," those monsters will come out and destroy you before you know what's happening—just like in the movie. In essence, working while being mentally unwell is like being in a quiet place. Talk too loudly about mental health, and you'll be destroyed. So, what have workplaces become? They've become a quiet place when it comes to mental health conditions. They've become a place where you commit career suicide if you speak about mental health. But why is this the case? Why have workplaces been so quiet and slow to address mental health crises? The answer is simple.

Stigma.

According to Mayo Clinic, stigma is when someone negatively views you because you have a distinguishing characteristic or personal trait that's thought to be, or is, a disadvantage (a negative stereotype). I have to admit, when I was diagnosed with bipolar disorder, I stigmatized myself—no help was needed. My diagnosis was equated to a death sentence in my mind. Nothing good could come from it.

During the time that I was hospitalized in a mental health facility, I tried to always remain calm because I certainly didn't want to end up in a strait jacket and be placed in a white room with padded walls (something I never witnessed during my time committed). Still, I do live in New York City, where the majority of the homeless population has a mental health disorder, and I was beginning to think homelessness might be my fate too. No one I heard about with a mental health condition was managing their mental illness with success, not even celebrities. You only heard about them when they suffered a mental health crisis publicly or had suddenly disappeared from the spotlight, or we learned of their death. Why would I be any different? How could I live with a mental illness and not suffer the same fate?

The self-imposed and societal stigma that I internalized is both familiar and dangerous. As a society, we have treated mental health and substance use disorders "as choices that can be controlled rather than as medical conditions that can be managed and treated. We isolate those suffering and create an atmosphere of blame and shame."[3]

When I reflected on those I knew with a mental illness, I remembered how hard it was to watch the movie *Mrs. Doubtfire* without wondering how the outrageously talented and brilliant Robin Williams could end up in such a fragile mental state that led him to take his life. I reflect on how the world is still shocked by the news that world traveler and chef Anthony Bourdain had taken his life. I also reflected on a crisp morning in June while driving to my office when I passed by an army of fire trucks and police cars on the Upper East Side of New York City, only to find out later that I was passing by the building where designer Kate Spade and had just taken her life. After her death, her husband Andy Spade wrote[4],

"Kate suffered from depression and anxiety for many years. She was actively seeking help and working closely with doctors to treat her disease, which takes far too many lives. We were in touch with her the night before, and she sounded happy. There was no indication and no warning that she would do this. It was a complete shock. And it clearly wasn't her. There were personal demons she was battling."

---

[3] Mental Health Is Just As Important As Your Physical Health, *Healthcare Home,* University of Utah Health, April 28, 2022, https://healthcare.utah.edu/healthfeed/postings/2022/04/mental-health-is-physical-health.php#:~:text=Unlike%20other%20physical%20illnesses%2C%20mental,the%20rest%20of%20your%20body, accessed on March 15, 2023.

[4] Cristi Carras, Kate Spade's Husband Issues Statement: She 'Suffered From Depression and Anxiety', Variety, June 6, 2018, https://variety.com/2018/biz/news/kate-spade-husband-death-statement-1202834789/.

A few weeks ago, the world was shocked again after learning that Stephen "tWitch" Boss had taken his life. tWitch, as we fondly called him, captured the hearts of people around the world as a contestant on *So, You Think You Can Dance*. After that, we watched his infectious smile on *The Ellen Show*. I had the opportunity of personally knowing him as he is from my hometown and attended my high school. I graduated before him, but we were both dancers growing up and ran in some of the same circles. His dancing career brightened the days of millions of people not just on Tik Tok but also on other social media platforms. I had just watched a TikTok video of him smiling and dancing posted just the day before he took his life. While the people who are close to these people know of their condition, those of us on the outside only see them as thriving, admirable, and extraordinarily successful people.

There are countless Cheslies, Anthonys, Kates, Robins, and tWiches around us, especially in our workplaces. While their close friends and relatives may know about their mental health conditions, they keep it guarded and quiet, allowing us who are on the outside to continue to think of them as close to perfection. We all know that perfection is a myth, unattainable, making the pursuit of it emotionally debilitating. I don't believe most people desire to strive for perfection, but the way the system is set up makes it seem as if there is no other choice—it's a path you have to take your opportunities on. And, with a known mental health condition, the perception of perfection is definitely out of reach. So, when you're suffering, it appears that you're only safe by remaining in a quiet place.

Consider this. One of your peers tells you that they have been diagnosed with cancer. Another informs you of their mental health disorder. Nine times out of ten, you know how to respond to the person with cancer way better than the person who informs you that they've been diagnosed with a mental health disorder. Why? Because we've been "programmed" to show empathy for someone with a cancer diagnosis. Everything we've seen and heard about cancer is that it is a disease that is most likely unpreventable, the person that has it is non-threatening, we can visibly see the pain and suffering that they are experiencing, and there may be a chance that person may not survive their diagnosis. That automatically evokes concern, worry, and the desire to support them in whatever way we can.

Even when watching movies, I've never seen a character diagnosed with cancer painted as harmful or a villain. I remember the first time I watched the movie *Stepmom*. Susan Sarandon played opposite Julia Roberts, who was her ex-husband's new, much younger girlfriend. Sarandon's character is mean and cruel to Robert's character no matter how hard Roberts tried to connect with her and her kids. The viewer feels sorry for Roberts because she just can't seem to compete with Sarandon, who is a "do no wrong" perfect mother. But your empathy immediately pivots when the viewer learns that Sarandon, spoiler alert, is secretly battling cancer. Now, Sarandon can do no wrong in anything. She has cancer, for Christ's sake! At the end of the movie, I cried as if Susan Sarandon's character was my very own mother and wail each time I watch it again. But life is not the movies. We are real people, not characters. And we, the people with mental health struggles, do not need tears. We need the support of people who are in positions of influence, and decision-making authority. We need allies to support us so we can get the services we need to better manage our lives.

My father was an alcoholic and a womanizer, present but not regularly active in my life. He was reticent and reserved, and when he was present in a room, everyone was cautious not to make too much noise. He would pick my sister and me up from dance school from time to time. I remember the embarrassment we would feel when we walked out the door to find him and the other parents sitting in their cars waiting for their kids. Only he would be inconspicuously turning up a bottle of whiskey. Sometimes we would ask if we could give our neighbor's kids a ride home, and he would not hesitate to agree. But, when we would all pile into the back seat of our 1985 Cadillac, we would find several empty bottles stacked across the floorboard. Most of them would be empty, but some would be filled with his urine. Everybody would pretend not to see those bottles, but my sister and I would sit in embarrassment.

Because of his lack of engagement as a father and his alcoholism, I never had feelings toward my father one way or another until one day—the day I got a dreaded call. Shortly after starting law school, my sister called me to let me know that my father had not only been diagnosed with cancer but was also on life support. He had undergone emergency surgery to remove part of his colon when the doctors found cancer in it, but because he also chain-smoked cigarettes, his lungs had collapsed post-op. Before going into surgery, he informed my family not to tell me about what was happening as he did not want to disrupt my studies. But it was time for me to know after his lungs collapsed and he was placed on life support. The moment I heard about my father's cancer diagnosis, my feelings suddenly shifted for my father. I loved him. I was concerned for him. I needed to be near him. I left school to be by his side for a couple of days. Eventually, my family encouraged me to return to school but it was so hard to do. I just didn't know if my time with him would be the last time I would see him. However, I had to keep on achieving my goals. We were fortunate that he fought and survived cancer for another eight years. During those eight years, we were closer than we had ever been. Alcoholism and his mental illness had torn us apart. Cancer brought us together.

Movies and the media aren't the only factors contributing to the stigma of mental health conditions and illnesses. Overcoming institutional stigma may be the toughest challenge to conquer. According to Pyschiatry.org[5] "Institutional stigma, is more

---

[5] Stigma, Prejudice and Discrimination Against People with Mental Illness, American Psychiatric Association, https://www.psychiatry.org/patients-families/stigma-and-discrimination, accessed March 15, 2023.

systemic, involving policies of the government and private organizations that intentionally or unintentionally limit opportunities for people with mental illness." It wasn't until my bipolar diagnosis that I realized how institutional stigma would impact my life in ways unimaginable.

I was one of the fortunate people that had access to healthcare when I experienced my mental health crisis. Don't assume that was enough by itself because it was not. Despite my access to mental health care and receiving adequate, unbiased help, I still had a lot to tend to, which meant my family did too. For instance, after I was discharged from the inpatient mental health facility, I was still not entirely well. I had done a ton of damage to my family and personal finances during my bipolar manic episode. I was still feeling the guilt, blame, and shame associated with my behavior and actions. It had been over a year since my manic episode, yet its ramifications were still raw and fresh for both me and my husband.

One of the biggest elephants in the room was the large amounts of money I gave out freely to strangers while in mania. This was the second time that this had happened in ten years. I was undiagnosed the first time and had no idea why I had done such a thing. Now, I know that this was a common symptom of being in a bipolar manic episode. I reflected on how my sister had lost her house, a couple of cars, jobs, and God knows what else as she battled her bipolar disorder. Although I was on medication and following my treatment plan, I was warned that there was still a chance that I would experience a bipolar manic episode in the future. I was desperate to protect my assets in case I did experience another manic episode.

In order to accomplish this, I decided that my best course of action was to be appointed a conservator to oversee my financial affairs. While this may seem like an extreme measure, I would learn that would mean I couldn't write a check, enter into any financial agreement, have a credit card, or even sign off on a job offer! But at that time, it seemed like the right thing to do. Naturally, I asked my trusted husband of many years to take on the responsibility of being my conservator. We already shared bank accounts, and what was mine was his, and what was his was mine. But, because I had been the one to handle our financial affairs, he didn't even notice the money was missing until it was too late. Although we were trying to protect ourselves from any danger that my illness may cause in the future, we didn't know that navigating the court system would be the most challenging issue of all, even though this was voluntary.

I believed that the court system would be on the side of protecting me from myself. Because the conservatorship was voluntary and my idea, I thought the process would be just a formality. My husband retained an attorney who informed him that these proceedings, usually referred to as guardianship, are primarily used to care for the elderly who could no longer care for themselves. He had also represented people my age struggling with mental health conditions. My husband was optimistic as the attorney walked him through the legal process until the attorney informed him that the court would reach out to my next of kin which meant my mother, sister, and son. My family would be interviewed by court-appointed representatives and asked their "opinions" on my husband being my conservator. This could not have come at a worse time. For one, my estranged sister had always reveled when I was at my worst and yet would be included in this process. She knew nothing of my life or my marriage. To give you an example of her distaste for me, my husband, kids, and I lived in Arkansas for six years. During that time, she never visited me or her niece or nephew (my children) even one time. Her daughter, who I had practically raised, would often spend her summer break with us. My sister would drive for ten hours to drop her off and not step one foot in our home but instead turn around and make the ten-hour drive back, just to avoid me. She would do the same thing when she picked her daughter up at the end of the summer. To this day, my daughter is not able to pick out her aunt from a group of strangers. Now, according to the attorney, my sister would have the opportunity to give her opinion about a serious matter in my life that she should not be involved in whatsoever in the first place!

I predicted that my mother's input would not be much better. After her divorce from my father when I was ten years old and the death of her parents soon after, I became her companion. When I met my husband, and she realized that we would probably get married, she knew she would lose me as her companion and automatically disliked my husband for this. Additionally, because of my sister's mental health condition, I was practically her only child, which meant I was solely responsible for her needs, whether it was including her in our family vacations, where she would spend the holidays or any other parental support. She was fresh from being upset that she had not been included in a family vacation to Europe and, of course, blamed my husband. However, her not coming was due to me setting my boundaries and needing time to be alone with my immediate family.

To make matters worse, as I stated earlier, this was also during the period when celebrity Britney Spears was seeking emancipation from her father's conservatorship, which made the whole process feel demeaning. All of these factors ended up in the hot mess we'd predicted they would after my family got involved. I had kept my family out of all aspects of my personal life for many years. Now, here they were knee deep in it. When the court representative interviewed me, she had already spoken to my mom, sister, and son. My son, who was attending college in the state where my sister and mom lived, had been influenced by them not to support the conservatorship. My mom and sister had defamed my husband and me so badly during the process that I have never spoken to them again. Ironically, they haven't spoken with me either. Perhaps it's guilt or shame, or perhaps they really don't care one bit. They also convinced my niece, who I had supported emotionally and financially for all of her life due to her mother's mental illness, to discard me. I realized that after forty-plus years of calling these people my family, they were just using me for their selfish reasons. As sad as it was to learn this, it was also liberating in a sense because I fully understood who I was dealing with, without the rose-colored glasses on, for the first time.

Now that I had boundaries that excluded some of the things that unjustly benefitted them, there was no reason for them to have me in their lives. I was at the most vulnerable time in my life and was abandoned by my flesh and blood. The conservatorship process had gotten so messy that we withdrew our petition from the court. We would need to find another way to protect me from me that didn't include involving so many other people.

Yet, despite what had been brought to light, this was only a few months after my suicide attempt, and it sent me spiraling back toward a dark place. I needed to get away from New York and be surrounded by loved ones. So, we decided to relocate for the summer to Lake Michigan, where my husband's large family was located, and also where we owned a boat that we could live on. Unfortunately, this move didn't completely circumvent my raw feelings of just going through the conservatorship process and being abandoned by my family. I found myself suicidal once again.

By this time, I was seeing a psychiatrist who accepted my medical insurance and the sessions seemed to be working out okay. Due to COVID-19, we had only been able to meet virtually, which worked out well, especially since we were temporarily in a different state. I would ask my husband to join in on my psych appointments as this allowed him to learn more about bipolar disorder and my treatment plan and share his perception of how I was doing. I had permitted him to call my psychiatrist if he thought I was in danger of harming myself or was experiencing a manic episode (when you're in mania, you're often in denial and need an outside intervention). He did have to call her a couple of times out of concern when I was very down, and she would prescribe something to help.

When I informed my psychiatrist that we had temporarily relocated to Michigan to live on our boat for the summer, she was concerned. "A boat?" she asked. I tried to reply with modesty that it was actually a two-bedroom, two-bath, 42 feet motor yacht (about the size of a New York apartment), but she was still concerned. I now have concluded there was some animosity that, as a White woman, she had never heard of a Black family owning and living on a yacht. From that time on, everything shifted. Her demeanor towards us changed, and she kept asking questions about the boat. Where is it? How big is it? Every time we spoke, she appeared more concerned with me living on a boat than providing me treatment for my mental health. Despite this feeling, I continued to seek treatment from her. But what happened next, I never would have guessed in a million years.

Still heartbroken by the abandonment of my family, I started ideating suicide again, and my husband and I quickly got her on a call to inform her of my feelings and to get advice on what to do next. When she learned that I was suicidal, she advised that we immediately go to the hospital, and we both agreed. As we were preparing to leave, my phone rang, and it was my psychiatrist. When I answered, she asked me if I was alone. I stated that I was as my husband was zipping up the boat, and I was in one of the staterooms in the cabin. She then went on to inform me that she had called the police to come and pick me up. Shocked, I asked, "Why?" She replied that she didn't trust that we were going to the hospital.

In my already frail state, I began to shake and cry. Then, she said, "There's more." My eyes widened in anticipation of what she could say next. She then informed me that she had called Child Protective Services (CPS). "What?!" I shouted. "What is going on?! I told you we were on our way to the hospital! My husband has six siblings living right here in this town who can care for my daughter. We will drop her off with one of them on our way! Why are you doing this?!" She had no answer—just silence. "There's more," she stated. My heart dropped. *Did you send a hitman*, I thought. "I put you on the 'Do Not Prescribe' list."

Those last words took the breath out of me. Then she added, "And by the way, I can no longer see you as a patient as you have left the state." With that, she hung up the phone.

This psychiatrist knew that I was already in a suicidal state of mind. She had no reason to believe that we wouldn't go to the hospital. We called her! And furthermore, she delivered all of this news to me purposefully out of the presence of my husband. WTF! I went to my husband and told him the news as quickly as possible. I was not going to be taken to the hospital by a police car! My daughter was at risk of being taken away from us simply because I was a harm to myself, not to others! He was as shocked as I was.

As soon as I delivered the news, we saw the local police marine vessel going up and down our marina, looking closely inside each boat. We knew they were looking for me. The police couldn't get into the marina because it's located behind a security gate, plus I never told my psychiatrist what slip we were in and what our boat's name was. We quickly grabbed our daughter and got off the boat as fast as we could. We dropped my daughter (a teenager, by the way, not a small child) at a relative's house and went straight to the hospital. We quickly informed someone to call the police and let them know we were there.

The medical staff was shocked when we shared what we had just experienced with our psychiatrist. They stated that they had never heard of someone calling CPS because a parent was suicidal, especially when another parent was around. The only conclusion that any of us could produce was that this mental health provider had a problem with a functioning, well-off Black family. I had heard of health disparities when it came to other medical conditions. I was shocked to learn how tennis great Serena Williams was treated during the birth of her daughter. Still, I never imagined in a million years that a trained mental health provider would allow her racial bias to make such bad decisions about an already fragile patient. So, now, here I was not only discarded and not supported by my family, but now I could not even protect myself through the court system or using a mental health provider.

My experience with institutional stigma didn't stop there.

Several months later, I finally applied for a TSA pre-check pass. With all the international traveling I've done over the past several years; you would have thought I would have already gained this credential. But, after standing in a security line at LaGuardia airport for almost an hour, I finally decided it was time. As I navigated through the application, everything seemed like the usual process of verifying my identity. "Where were you born?" "Have you gone by another name?" "Have you been convicted of a felony?" Then came a question that stopped me in my tracks. Question #6 read, in part, *Have you been involuntarily committed to an inpatient facility for mental health or psychiatric reasons?* As you know, my answer was "yes." At the top of the form, it clearly stated that if you answered "yes" to question 6, *you may want to reconsider applying.* What?! So, because at one point in my life, I attempted to harm myself and received the medical treatment that I needed, I can't keep my shoes on at the airport while going through security! On this TSA application, the only other questions included with this one asked about felony convictions. According to the United States Government, if you have served time in a psychiatric facility, you may as well have gone to prison and have a record that will follow you for the rest of your life. Unbelievable!

I'll survive going through long security lines at the airport and taking my shoes off at security. I've been doing it for years. It doesn't lessen the disappointment though, especially when you think about how you've invested years into your education, training, and career just for your non-threatening mental illnesses to hold you back. Studies by Duke University have shown that people in the legal and medical professions have some of the highest rates of mental illnesses, and those numbers are only the reported cases[6]. In reality, the numbers are much higher. Why? Because we're fighting a war that we didn't even know we were in. Get this. To become licensed in these professions, legal or medical, in many states, the licensing agencies most often ask several intrusive questions about your mental health and history. If you answer that you have received treatment for a mental health disorder, you could be deemed incompetent to work in your profession and lose your career altogether. Institutional and public stigmas may be as obvious as the nose on your face or so subtle that you wonder if they do exist at times…until they are not subtle any longer because something happens, such as the loss of a job.

So, where does the stigma of mental health leave us? We remain mostly quiet in our homes, communities, and workplaces, eager to not be targeted or the topic of someone else's conversation. We also know something that those not suffering do not know *being diagnosed with a mental health condition is terrifying*. Even when you're treated, doing well, and non-threatening to yourself or others, you are afraid of the next barrier or obstacle you'll face that's outside of your control. What makes matters worse is the slow creep of anticipation for that next manic moment to arrive.

What if we, the crazies, instead had an opportunity to show what makes us, the unordinary, extraordinary? What if we were no longer in a quiet place and used our voices and actions to break the stigma of mental illness?

---

[6] James TR Jones, "High Functioning": Successful Professionals With Severe Mental Illness, Duke Law School, https://scholarship.law.duke.edu/cgi/viewcontent.cgi?article=1056&context=dflsc , accessed March 15, 2023.

CHAPTER 3

CRAZY-ISH

It's been two years since I was diagnosed with bipolar disorder. As I've learned more through researching my condition, I've come to realize that the negative impact of my condition is minimal in my life, compared to others I've talked to. Don't get me wrong; it still feels like a giant weight looming over my head often enough.

Over the span of my forty-plus years of living, I've had about three manic episodes and experienced about three bouts of severe depression. When I was in hypomania, I worked long and hard and felt extremely happy about life. Despite not having a bipolar diagnosis, I did show symptoms of the condition in my early twenties. Thankfully, these symptoms did not deter me from maintaining a successful marriage, raising two wonderful kids, and having a thriving career.

Behind all of my success and happiness, a different story played out at times. There were situations in which life dealt me a tough hand, and those experiences also impacted my mental health. Since I've been diagnosed with bipolar disorder, it's been challenging to distinguish between when I'm experiencing a bipolar episode or just poor mental health. There is, however, a distinct difference between the two, and it's vital to understand what that is.

When I shared about my father passing away from cancer, I didn't share the full story. There's more to it. A couple of years before his death, I had been relocated from Arkansas to New York for work. Like many who move to New York, it was far more expensive to live there than I could ever have imagined. The company had only given me a five percent cost of living increase which wasn't nearly enough to live on. I loved the company and the work I was doing, but I and my family struggled financially. So, it was no surprise that when I received a call from an executive recruiter about a Director of Talent position at a prominent healthcare organization, I jumped at the opportunity to work for a NY-based company that would pay a NY salary. After going through the interview process, I proudly accepted an offer for nearly $50,000 more than I was currently making. Life was about to become good!

Just a few days before my start date, I received a call from my father informing me that his eight-year cancer battle had ended and he was going to be placed in hospice care. He was given about six weeks to live, which left me feeling devastated. He was in Alabama, and we had just begun to forge a father-daughter relationship. I hesitantly called my new boss and asked if I could push my start date back by two weeks so I could spend some time with my father during his last weeks before starting my new role. She agreed.

After returning to New York and beginning my new job, my mind was preoccupied with the fact that I would likely never see my father again. But I needed to make an excellent first impression. So, I put my emotions on the back burner and went all in to prove my worth at my new job. This job felt very different from my previous one, which gave me tons of autonomy and flexibility. Although I was at the director level, it felt like I was new to my profession. Plus, I was the third Director of Talent that had been hired, creating animosity between myself and the other two directors. Why was I there? What were our distinctive functions? From the very start, there was no structure or framework provided by the VP and this added to the tension from the get-go. Also, did I mention I had a two-and-a-half-hour commute one way each day?

I found myself making more money but barely surviving. Every workday I was up at 5:00 AM for a two-plus hour drive on the Long Island Expressway. I'd start work and it was always intense and competitive from start to finish. In the back of my mind I was worried that at any moment, I would get a call that my dad was gone. Did I also mention that I was a wife and mother? But thank goodness, I have a wonderful, supportive, stay-at-home husband who took care of the domestic stuff. Otherwise, I would not have been able to do the job.

I thought that by having a female boss and female colleagues I would receive empathy and compassion for my current situation. Nothing could have been further from the truth. Everyone was cutthroat, rigid, and non-compassionate. Although they knew my father was in hospice care with just weeks to live, no one asked about him, so I didn't even mention him or anything non-work related. I had never felt so disconnected from a team.

On August 12th, I spoke with my father on my way to work. He sounded great and chipper. Later that day, my phone rang with an Alabama number. It was his hospice nurse. His organs were shutting down. If I wanted to see him again, I needed to get to Alabama immediately. I called my boss and told her I needed to leave; however, I couldn't get a flight out until early the next morning. As my husband and I were loading the car with my suitcase and heading to the airport at about 3:30 AM, my phone rang again. I knew what that meant. He was gone.

For the next few days, my sister and I arranged his funeral. Although I was on unpaid bereavement leave (yes, unpaid because I hadn't worked 90 days yet), I was still checking and responding to emails. I even found myself checking emails on the way to his funeral. Not once did my boss discourage me from doing this. She just kept the emails coming and accepted my responses. Additionally, my father left his entire estate to me, so I needed to stay in Alabama for just a couple more days to get some of the affairs in order and to shut down his house. But then I got the dreaded call. "Natasha, when are you coming back to work?" I dropped everything and headed back to New York. Not only was I not paid for the time I was gone (I needed the money, and I also had quasi-worked while I was on leave), but no one even hugged me or asked how I was doing upon my return. For the "team," it was business as usual, which meant no sense of compassion either. That was the norm.

What I experienced at that job during a tough time was common. Eventually, I cried on the way to work and dreaded walking through the doors. Although my previous job would have responded in a more compassionate and empathetic way, I had traded off a great work culture for a better salary. At that time, I was not diagnosed with a mental illness and wasn't presenting symptoms of bipolar disorder, but my mental health was suffering due to my work environment.

According to the Centers for Disease Control (CDC), mental illness is "conditions that affect a person's thinking, feeling, mood, or behavior." These can include but aren't limited to depression, anxiety, bipolar disorder, or schizophrenia. Mental health reflects "our emotional, psychological, and social well-being," affecting "how we think, feel, and act." It substantially impacts how we interact with others, handle problems, and make decisions[7].

During this time, I wasn't in a depressive state, but I dreaded going to work, had difficulty connecting with my colleagues, and was

---

[7] Yes, There is a Big Difference Between Mental Health and Mental Illness, *Putting People First In Mental Health,* Mass General Brigham McLean, https://www.mcleanhospital.org/essential/mental-health-mental-illness, accessed March 15, 2023.

always on the "edge" about what my boss might say or do. When I wasn't at work, I was fine. I was happy with my family and enjoyed my time with them. I sometimes contemplated if I was making stuff up about how I felt about my job. I would ask questions of myself like, "with a higher title and salary can you really expect a healthy work environment?" That battle in my head played on for years, although my situation at work only worsened. The expectations and demands unjustifiably intensified. Work-life balance (whatever that is) was non-existent (especially with the timely commute). The unhealthy competition that was encouraged between my peers and me ultimately impacted our ability to perform as a team. I was unhappy, unmotivated, and burned out. This had nothing to do with my bipolar diagnosis but had everything to do with bad management and an unhealthy work environment. Sometimes, I felt crazy for staying in such an environment for so long, but I wasn't crazy. I was crazy-ish.

Healthy and psychologically safe work environments are hard to come by, with many of us making the tough decision to work in environments that are healthy and safe, but with a trade-off sometimes of lower salaries or no advancement or we have a high title and salary, but the environment sucks. Whatever the case, be it dreading walking into work or dreading opening your mail knowing your salary won't cover the cost of the bills that await, that dread is a symptom of something that is taking its toll on you. Functioning day-to-day at work becomes something that you feel is impossible to achieve with a modicum of success. Gone are those moments of the optimistic achiever you once felt like you were. Believe me, I know.

The cycle of going from being an HR executive at a mental health hospital to becoming a patient at another mental health hospital and going back to being to an HR executive at at the first mental health hospital was an eye-opening experience for me. Because there are two mental health hospitals involved in this story, I will refer to the hospital that I worked in as "MHA" and the one I was hospitalized in as "MHB". As the Chief Human Resources Officer at MHA, this was the first time in my career that I believed

I didn't have to trade off a great work culture for great pay and benefits. I loved working with my boss, who was the CEO. Notice, I used the word "with" not "for"? That's because we had a wonderful collaborative working relationship with mutual respect and shared goals. He allowed me to be authentic and I felt seen, valued, and heard, which isn't always the case working in corporate America. He even supported my decision to run a consulting and speaking business on the side while working at the hospital full-time. I was exceeding the goals he laid out for me; that was the only thing that mattered. For four years, I was in "work heaven." I am told that when I came back to consciousness after I overdosed, he was the first person I called (I don't remember doing so to this day). But he made sure that I was sent immediately to MHB and received first-class service, which I did.

While I was a patient at MHB, I feared how my life would change once I was discharged. As the days went by, I didn't even want to be discharged as the facility had become my safe place. How would I explain to my clients and my social media followers where I had been and what I had been diagnosed with? Every time I looked in the mirror, a "crazy lady" was staring back at me. Was that what others were seeing, too, I wondered? But the one thing I didn't feel quite as uneasy about what losing my value at work. My boss knew me. We had worked together for four years. OUR WORK WAS MENTAL HEALTH! I was probably in the best position that anyone else who had just been diagnosed with a severe mental health condition could be in as it related to returning to work.

At MHB, we were given access to iPads during the day to watch movies, FaceTime with our families and friends (which was great since visits were limited due to COVID-19) or do just about anything else (but it didn't have a camera or video capabilities). I would often check in with my boss. Not to check in on work, but because he was my friend.

One day he asked if I felt well enough to join an important, but quick work meeting. My stomach dropped. I knew he would never ask me to join a work meeting while I was hospitalized at MHB unless it was something really, really important. I agreed. I was right. On the call, he announced that he was leaving the MHA for another position within the health system. After the call was over, I called him back and bawled my eyes out. He knew what I was thinking and just sat there and listened to me cry. Even he couldn't come up with comforting words to say.

Once discharged, I entered a partial hospitalization program for the next few months, then returned to work full-time remotely. I came back just in time to bid my boss farewell via Zoom. It was hard to watch him go on to his next opportunity with fear lurking inside of me about who would replace him. Who would I need to prove myself to just coming from a suicide attempt, inpatient hospitalization, and bipolar diagnosis? This was the worst time in the world for me to have such a significant change in my life. However, my worries subsided a little when my new boss was finally revealed. The chairman of the Board of Directors of MHA, who was also a licensed psychiatrist at one of the top health systems in the U.S., would be my new boss. He knew me and my capabilities. I was relieved…for about a day.

The first red flag was that he did not support me working remotely full-time. I didn't understand the pushback to this accommodation as at that time all meetings were done via video. I would have to arrive at my office (which was not even located in the hospital building) and sit in front of my computer screen all day, just as I would do at home. The second red flag was that the person covering for me during my leave of absence did not go away upon my return which would usually happen when someone else returned. In fact, I was told we would be splitting my duties, but there was no clear direction on how. This confused us, my team, and my internal clients. The third red flag was that my new boss refused to meet with me without the presence of the Chief People Officer of the entire health system. I had a dotted line reporting structure to him, but this was never the case with my old boss. My work life had been officially flipped upside down.

It became apparent to me that my stellar reputation as the head of HR at the MHA had been tainted. Maybe they felt they were doing me a favor by keeping on the person covering for me as "help" so I wouldn't be overwhelmed. Or maybe my new boss was afraid of saying the wrong thing to a person who was now diagnosed with a mental health condition, and that's why he wanted someone else present. I would also learn that my new boss just didn't think remote work was ideal in a hospital setting, whether you were patient-facing or not. Whatever the case was, my perception was that my work life had changed significantly from before I was diagnosed with a mental health condition.

I felt incapable, incompetent, and quite frankly embarrassed. I felt terrible for my team, who I adored and who adored me, yet they were torn between two bosses. Eventually, I expressed my concerns about splitting my role with someone else to the Chief People Officer. I told him how this decision was being perceived by myself and others. The person that filled in for me mysteriously disappeared just as quickly as she appeared after that conversation, but things never really improved between my new boss and me. Unbelievably, it got worse. One of the final straws was when my boss reprimanded me during my performance evaluation for sharing my mental health journey with a hospital surveyor. If you're unfamiliar with the healthcare industry, hospitals are often surveyed by agencies to put in simple terms, "make sure they are doing sh*t right." These visits (most of the time unannounced) are a big deal in healthcare, and we spend months preparing for them. The fewer citations or violations, the better! When the surveyors visit, they ensure that all the laws and regulations are being followed, that the facilities are safe and clean, and that the people who work there are qualified, certified, and licensed to be in their profession. The last part fell under my responsibility. As I was meeting with the surveyor, I was bragging about what an excellent hospital MHA was and all the fantastic things we did for our patients and staff. I wanted to share my perspective as an employee and a former patient at MHB. The surveyor enjoyed the conversation and gave me accolades for my time with her publicly.

But my boss didn't appreciate me sharing my experience as a patient and told me that it could have "backfired." He didn't share how and I didn't ask. I got the point. Stop talking about being *crazy*. The most hurtful thing was as a psychiatrist, he never even asked me how I was doing after I returned from my leave. I couldn't help but reflect on when I was out with COVID-19, and he sent me the most beautiful flowers. But bipolar disorder got nothing but shame, embarrassment, and humiliation. Maybe I perceived the whole thing wrong. Maybe I was crazy to think I could return to my workplace of four years like my mental health crisis didn't happen. Or just perhaps I was crazy-ish. I'll never know.

I worked at MHA for another year before deciding that I just needed to say goodbye. I was back in that dreaded place I had been before. I was trading off psychological safety for income stability and medical insurance. My bipolar disorder was under control, but my mental health was waning. It was a slippery slope that I wasn't willing to go down. I was much smarter now, and I knew where that could lead me. I had placed new boundaries for myself, and they were being crossed daily. To this day, I reflect, wondering if I really should have walked out on such a high-profile, high-paying job after five years. They didn't ask me to leave. I received an "exceeds expectations" on my final performance review. When I tell people what I left on the table when I left, they respond, "girl, are you crazy!?"

Yep. I'm CRAZY AF.

PART II

Crazy

&

FIGHTING

Winston Churchill is regarded as one of the most influential leaders in history. As the Prime Minister of Great Britain during both World Wars I and II, he solidified his icon legacy by leading Britain from the brink of defeat to victory. However, as a middle-aged man, he was diagnosed with bipolar disorder. His bipolar manic episodes fueled his ability to lead one of the world's most powerful nations through wars, and he managed to write over 43 books while doing so. He was known to recede from mania to depression, which became known to his friends and acquaintances as his "black dog." But he always found a way to push through and keep fighting. Winston Churchill was CRAZY AF: CRAZY And Fighting, and at this point in my story, so was I.

CHAPTER 4

PSYCHOLOGICAL WARFARE

When I left my c-suite job, I was already being recognized as a top voice for workplace mental health as I publicly shared my journey as someone living, working, and running a business with bipolar disorder. I knew that being a workplace mental health advocate would be my new calling. Not because of any accolades I had received, but because working with a mental illness and promoting mental health in the workplace was still a taboo subject, yet one my life revolved around in many ways.

Over the past few years, celebrities such as Jennifer Lewis, Taraji P. Henson, Selena Gomez, Oprah Winfrey, Michael Phelps, Carson Daily, and Big Sean have spoken openly about their mental health struggles. Simon Biles and Naomi Osaka have even gone so far as to opt out of major events and media appearances, citing their desire to protect their mental health. I applaud all of these people and many others for their willingness to use their platforms to destigmatize mental illness. However, is this same ability to be vulnerable and transparent about mental health issues available to your average, everyday worker? The answer is a resounding no.

Meet Kevin Berling.

Kevin asked his manager not to throw him a birthday party as his employer did for every employee. Kevin explained that the reason that he didn't want a birthday party was not that he was a party pooper, but rather because the event might cause him immense stress and maybe even a panic attack. Well, guess what? His manager threw that birthday party anyway. As predicted, Kevin had a panic attack and left the party. From his car, he texted his boss how upset he was that his request wasn't accommodated.

What do you think happened next? Well, what should have happened was for his manager to meet with Kevin to apologize for not following his wishes and use this incident as a learning opportunity to not only respect the wishes of his employee but to learn more about mental health conditions and how they present themselves in the workplace. But that didn't happen. Instead, Kevin's boss and other company representatives met with him all right. Still, it wasn't to apologize or learn about his condition and what they could do to prevent Kevin from having another work-related panic attack. Instead, the meeting was used to chastise him for his behavior of leaving the party, which included remarks such as that he was "stealing his co-workers' joy" and that he was "being a little girl." Yes, you read that right.

After this meeting, you can probably guess what happened next. Kevin suffered another panic attack. This time, there was no follow-up meeting. He was fired from his job a couple of days later. And get this: he was fired for "workplace violence." Yes, you read that right, too. He was fired because his panic attacks were perceived as acts of violence. Kevin was awarded nearly $500,000.00 for his rights under the Americans with Disabilities Act (a.k.a. the ADA, which we will discuss further in the book) and for retaliation. $300,00.00 of that award was for the emotional stress that the company put on him during these unfortunate events.

I think Kevin's birthday party will go down as the most expensive office birthday party of all time. But I couldn't care less about what Kevin's company had to pay him. I care about Kevin. Imagine what it was like for him to go through these events. I can just imagine that instead of being excited about his birthday, he had to feel fear because he knew that his company likes to throw birthday parties which triggered panic attacks for him. Kevin was courageous to inform his manager about his mental health condition. Many of us don't have that courage, which triggers mental health issues that we hide from our employers. Remember my story of reporting to jury duty and suffering, which I now know was probably a panic attack? I didn't dare to tell my boss what was happening, which led to my eventual termination. Kevin was simply attempting to avoid a mental health trigger. He didn't do anything wrong. All he did was make a reasonable request that would protect his mental health and he got fired for it...for not wanting a birthday party.

When protecting our mental health in the workplace, we are in psychological warfare with our organizations. Psychological warfare, as described by history expert Robert Longley, is a "non-lethal effort to capture hearts and minds. It typically employs propaganda to influence the values, beliefs, emotions, reasoning, motives, or behavior of its targets."[8] Most organizations use psychological warfare to lure appealing candidates into their workplaces by making promises of strong and inclusive work cultures, great benefits, and growth opportunities. As an HR leader, I have sat directly across from job candidates, touting how great a company is to work for, all while crossing my fingers behind my back. Sometimes, I would go so far as to share my own (fake) positive experience working there. If I did not fill the open

---

[8] Robert Longley, An Introduction to Psychological Warfare, ThoughtCo, Updated October 22, 2019, https://www.thoughtco.com/psychological-warfare-definition-4151867.

position, I was not being successful in my role. So, I needed to get that candidate to say "yes" to my offer by any means necessary. I would engage in psychological warfare by asking the candidate what they were looking for in a position and from an organization. Then, I would go on and on about how my company could offer all those things, plus more! But the truth was, everything I said was just a bunch of bologna. All of the things that the candidate wanted from this opportunity were all of the things that the current employees wished they had. Yeah, these perks, benefits, and culture statements all looked good on paper, but they were just pies in the skies.

We've all seen those pharmaceutical commercials where the medication being advertised will supposedly help you resolve or at least get some form of relief from a medical condition. But at the end of the commercial, there is a long list of side effects in small print i.e., blurry vision, hearing loss, paralysis, amnesia, and a broken toe. My daughter and I laugh every time we hear this and joke that we might as well just deal with the original condition! Well, when making a job offer to a candidate, instead of including the whole "we are an equal employment opportunity" crap statement on the job offer, we should include a warning message that reads:

WARNING: This job offer may come with some severe side effects. Some people who have accepted this position in the past reported low morale, long hours, loss of vacation and sick time, belittling, harassment, a touch of racism, burnout, and increasing signs of depression. If you experience any of these things, don't report them to me because I will make you feel like you're making shit up in your head."

All kidding aside, the workplace propaganda of creating psychological warfare with their workforce is rampant, but during the COVID-19 pandemic, folks started to catch on to the facade. As people across the world were called into quarantine, prompting the majority of the population to have the opportunity to work remotely, the curtain was pulled back on the false realities of work.

For decades, workers begged for the elusive work-life balance. Time and time again, they were told that working from home was not possible. I can't even begin to count the number of times in my career when my day was filled with listening in to conference calls on mute and thinking, *I got all dressed up for work today just to sit at my desk and join hundreds of other people on mute to listen to just a few people talk while I scroll through Instagram.* But when organizations had no choice but to shift to remote work, magic happened overnight. Laptops were shipped. Zoom accounts were set up. Pajama bottoms became the new black. Although everyone was uncertain and afraid of what this virus could do and how long it would last, for most, there was comfort in being home.

Home became a safe place, not just from the coronavirus but from toxic work environments. Many people didn't realize just how their workplaces were impacting their mental health until they had the opportunity to step away from them. Remote work creates a natural buffer that allows for less time for those little annoyances from your boss and coworkers, especially for those of us from marginalized groups. The sneaky, microaggressive comments about your hair, accent, and the food you eat, were suddenly missing from your life. You found yourself being able to get your work done while also re-engaging in the things you love outside of work, too (remember those?). In addition to avoiding frustrating coworkers, people could sleep more, save money, spend more time with family, and work in flexible physical spaces that are more conducive to mental well-being. More importantly, remote work gave people in marginalized communities a break from the psychological distress associated with their identities.

Meet Barbie.

Barbie is an accomplished human resources executive, a middle-aged white, gay woman. Over the past couple of years, she's also become a friend. I've had the opportunity to meet her lovely wife and their two beautiful kids. Over lunch one day, she shared with me the particular burden of being a gay woman at work that I'd never thought of before: "having to come out of the closet Every.

Single. Day." During day-to-day conversations at work, workers often talk about their families. However, when people speak to her about her family, they often refer to her spouse as her husband. She then has to inform them that she has a wife. Once they find out that she and her wife have children, the curiosity crescendos to "how." She told me that people are shameless when asking about her personal life in a way that they would never ask a cisgender, heterosexual person. She psychologically prepares herself every day for the possibility to have to explain her sexual orientation and familial status. During quarantine, Barbie was laid off from her c-suite job and so started her own consulting business. Now that she works remotely, she mostly avoids those conversations. This gives her space to focus on her work and clients rather than having to explain her personal life.

The year 2020 brought a global pandemic, but, in the same year, the murder of a man by the name of George Floyd brought a racial reckoning to workplaces across America. Finally recognizing the systemic barriers that have been oppressing Black people in the workplace, organizational leaders made unprecedented commitments to dismantle these systems and provide more equitable work environments. However, several years later, these commitments to Black employees seemingly diminished. In fact, in some cases, these commitments weren't commitments at all. They were veiled attempts to follow "the flavor of the month" or, to be more politically correct, to do it because everybody else was.

One glaring example was when the former NFL Coach for the Miami Dolphins was a candidate for the head coaching job for the New York Giants. Brian Flores, a Black man, was scheduled to interview for the New York Giants head coaching job. But before his interview, he received a text message from Bill Belichick — his former boss with the Patriots — that mistakenly informed him that the Giants had already decided to hire Brian Daboll. Belichick appeared to be under the impression he was texting Daboll and attempted to congratulate him on the hire. Whew, text messages will get you every time!

It appeared that the Giants were just complying with the "Rooney Rule" enacted by the NFL, which requires teams to interview at least two minority candidates for head coaching and football operations jobs. Although this rule was enacted to ensure that underrepresented applicants have an opportunity to sit down with owners of the teams, to most of the teams, it's just a check-the-box exercise. The Rooney Rule is another example of psychological warfare organizations engage in with their employees. It makes you think you have a chance when you're not even in the running. Rules, policies, diversity statements, and commitments are put in place to give the illusion that they care or want to do the right thing, but in fact, it's just a play on the emotions of their workforce, and that is dangerous. Decades of research show us that when employees are "chronically treated differently, unfairly, or badly" they most often go on to suffer from "effects ranging from low self-esteem to a higher risk for developing stress-related disorders such as anxiety and depression."[9]

All of this ties back into psychological warfare. A company may agree upon what they need to meet a criterion, and they may say they are part of the solution, but if it's words without actions, it has zero value. And surely, if you cannot get people in an organization to understand the calling and its benefits, how are they going to contribute to positive change in the workplace? It becomes smoke and mirrors, kind of like my son when he was little and promised to behave, then turning around and doing

---

[9] Jess Maynard, Alarmingly high rates of workplace discrimination are leading to depression, Spring Health, https://springhealth.com/blog/workplace-discrimination-and-depression/#:~:text=A%20large%2C%20peer%2Dreviewed%20study,%2C%20and%20%20pronounced%20depressive%20symptoms.%E2%80%9D.

something that made me feel that he had definitely not been behaving, whatever that really means.

As the world continues to stabilize from the COVID-19 pandemic, it has become clear that organizations can no longer engage in psychological warfare with their employees. Their employees are on to their performative efforts. Budgets for diversity, equity, and inclusion programs have dwindled. There have been little to no recognizable additions noted other than shifts back to the old way of doing things that have taken hold, including eliminating remote work. Catchphrases like "quiet quitting" demonstrate how the tables have turned. Employees are showing up for work and doing their jobs, but at the same time, they are no longer going over and beyond to ensure the organization's success. They show up, do their job, collect their paychecks, and go home.

CHAPTER 5

FAKE IT TILL YOU MAKE IT

I've often read quotes from the *Art of War* by Sun Tzu, although, I'll admit, I haven't read the entire book. I first became interested in Tzu's philosophies when I began running a business and realized how competitive and cutthroat it could sometimes be. I don't think I have ever applied any of his principles, but during that beginning stage after being diagnosed with a mental illness, his words began to ring true. At this point in my mental health journey, I was not confident I would win this battle. To "win" meant that I could return to my pre-mental health crisis state. I could go back to being an accomplished professional and check off my goals individually. Although I would still be *crazy*, no one would know. Just like it always had been. It was an illusion—people did know. I had let the cat out of the bag with my forthrightness and I wanted to get people talking, sure, but not about me as much as the challenges with mental health that we were up against. Still, the thought entered my mind at times to stop talking about it, hoping that others would forget too. They didn't like talking about this stuff anyway, right?

What was going on? I was beginning to doubt my ability to change the conversation about mental health and my ability to help others. At this point in my battle, there was one piece of advice from Sun Tzu that I took to head,
"Appear weak when you are strong, and strong when you are weak."

As I dwelled on this quote, I interpreted it as "fake it till you make it."

As I alluded to earlier, my sister and I have never been close. She resented me being born because she was no longer the only grandchild on our paternal side, which she had been for seven years. When I was born, that ruined "everything" for her. At least that's what she told me as an explanation as to why she never could seem to get her life completely together. Growing up, she was beautiful and talented and was well on her way to becoming Miss Alabama as a young adult. However, somehow that dream phased out. As the years passed, she would get these great jobs, excel in her roles, then lose them. She would have great friends and lose them too. She couldn't explain her destructive behavior. She couldn't explain that every time she got her life together, she would somehow make sure it all came crashing down.

I remember distinctively my niece calling me one day, frantic as the car that my father had just purchased for her was missing from the parking lot of her apartment. When she called her mom to tell her it had been stolen, my sister informed her that it had not been stolen, rather she had pawned it for cash and couldn't pay the loan back, so the loan sharks took the car. Another incident involved her embezzling funds from my niece's elite private school in which she had been enrolled since kindergarten and my sister had worked there just as long. After they discovered her misdeeds, they fired my sister and expelled my niece right before she was to start high school. My sister's destructive behavior became increasingly worse as time progressed, and she was slowly but surely losing the trust and support of her loved ones.

One day my mom called and told me she needed to talk to me. Her voice was just about as serious as I've ever heard it. I pulled up to her apartment, and she got in the car, took a deep breath, and told me my sister had cancer. My first instinct was to laugh. My mom looked at me with shock and disgust. "You believe that!?" I replied. It was at that moment, she realized the truth. She dropped her head down in embarrassment that she could have ever fallen for her eldest daughter's story. But it was too late; word had spread and the whole family had been called. The prayer warriors were in full effect. Who was gonna tell them that this was just another one of my sister's facades? I called my dad to tell him I didn't believe my sister had cancer. Since he had been battling cancer for years at that point, he was less hesitant to agree with my conclusion. Instead, he called and asked me to accompany my sister to her next chemo appointment. My sister, however, said she would rather go through chemo "alone."

That's when he knew, too, of her deceit. She was scheduled to go to chemo on a Tuesday. My father secretly sat in the cancer center's parking lot from the moment it opened until it almost closed, waiting for her to arrive, hoping we were all wrong. She never did. At this point, he had been a patient there for years and had developed close relationships with many of the nursing staff there. He finally found a nurse he was comfortable confiding in and asked her to do an unthinkable favor. "Look to see if my daughter is a patient here," he said. The nurse did the favor. The answer was no.

I don't share this story to paint my sister as a bad person, although, for many years, that was my only conclusion. Truth was, she was sick and didn't know how to explain it. She couldn't explain her actions. She couldn't explain her destructive behavior. She couldn't explain that every time she got her life together, she would somehow make sure it all came crashing down. Her life was spiraling with each passing year, and with each year, she lost more people. She had no answers for her behavior. She needed support. She needed something to get empathy, sympathy, and concern, so she faked cancer. It was way easier than saying, I'm worried I might not be mentally well. Years later, she, too, would be diagnosed with bipolar disorder. Although we have the same diagnosis, so far, our outcomes have been different. But what is the same was that during our mental health journeys, we had no explanation for how we were feeling, so we both faked it until we made it. In other words, we ignored the blaring signs of our mental illnesses until we had no other choice.

In the previous chapter, I shared the story of coach Brian Flores who showed up to an interview for an NFL head coach position that was already filled. When he was asked why he still went to the interview despite getting the infamous text that the job had already been filled, he eloquently responded with "the audacity of hope." He was hoping that the text he received was wrong. He was hoping that he did have a chance at this opportunity. He was hoping that everything would turn out fine. But he was wrong. The same was true for Kevin Berling, who hoped his boss would understand his concerns about having a birthday party and not throw him one. He hoped that by being honest about his condition, he would forge an easier path to maintain his mental health.

When it comes to mental health, many have been depending on the *audacity of hope*.

"I hope that one day my boss puts in her resignation so I can stop dreading coming to work."

"I hope that one day, my employer sees the value that I bring to this company so that I will be paid equitably."

"I hope no one says anything offensive today so I can just do my job and not be distracted."

"I hope they fill that vacancy today so I can stop being burned out."

"I hope I can take all of my vacations this year."

"I hope no one finds out about my mental health diagnosis."

When you're struggling with your mental health, it feels easier to hide it and keep drudging along as if nothing is happening. All these "I hope" statements are what get you by. And others often don't mind that you are doing that either, because it is often easier to ignore the challenge or separate yourself from it by distancing yourself from the person. Either way, our reluctance to address mental health, especially in the workplace, has created a crisis that will take an insurmountable amount of time to reconcile.

Once I made my mental health journey public, the people I worked with during that time were in shock. Not only because I had just publicly come out as mentally ill, but because many of them had been working with me on a day-to-day basis, and I showed no indication that I was in crisis. My consulting business was in full swing in June of 2020 as many of my clients were full speed ahead preparing their DEI strategies. They had no idea that as they worked with me, I was in a full-blown bipolar manic episode. Behind the scenes, my mind was ultimately out of control. I was plotting to leave my family, quit my profession, and start an Only Fans account. I'm not lying! I was giving away money left and right. Talking at the speed of light. And I might have jumped off the Brooklyn Bridge just for funsies. I also engaged in terrible, destructive behavior that I'm not ready to talk about publicly yet. But, yes, that's what it's like being in a manic episode. By the time Fall came around, I had crashed. I was no longer in mania but was in a bipolar depressive state. I was in a place of guilt and shame for all the things I had done while in mania. In the days leading to my suicide attempt, I was on Zoom calls smiling and engaging as usual, but when I left the video room, I was in a place of despair, loneliness, and sadness.
Now that organizations are acknowledging the mental health crisis, I've seen so much advice put out as to what to look for to determine if an employee needs help. The most common signs I see are:
- appears to be sad
- low productivity

- high absenteeism
- changes in mood

All of these symptoms are, certainly, symptoms to look out for and address but they are only the tip of the iceberg. There is so much more to it, as mental health includes our emotional, psychological, and social well-being. Just because you have poor mental health doesn't mean you have a mental illness. And just because you have a mental illness doesn't mean you don't have good mental health. I get why this can seem confusing. Think of mental health as a spectrum that ranges from mental wellness to mental suffering. Everyone at any time falls somewhere on that spectrum. You may mean that you're doing mentally well coping with the everyday stressors of life, you may be feeling exhausted and burned out, and you may be in crisis mode and having difficulty getting through the day. You can think of a spectrum of starting with green, moving to yellow and orange, and ending with red. The problem is that many of us, especially as we navigate our workplaces, fall on the yellow, orange, and red parts of the spectrum, but present ourselves as green. Why? Well, let's explore that.

The first and obvious answer is the stigma which we've already discussed. But there are other reasons, as well. Many people are in denial that they need mental health care. After I started exhibiting signs of bipolar mania, my husband recognized that my speech had sped up and that my eyes were glazed. He kept asking me if "I was okay." I became more offended each time he asked. I was adamant that I was just fine, although I knew I was having intrusive, unusual thoughts. I've learned that the scientific definition of rejecting your mental illness is called anosognosia. According to NAMI[10], "brain imaging studies have shown that

---

[10] Anosognosia, National Alliance on Mental Illness, https://www.nami.org/About-Mental-Illness/Common-with-Mental-Illness/Anosognosia, accessed March 15, 2023.

this crucial area of the brain can be damaged by schizophrenia and bipolar disorder as well as by diseases like dementia. When the frontal lobe isn't operating at 100%, a person may lose—or partially lose—the ability to update his or her self-image." Because we didn't get the "update" about ourselves, we are in true denial. We become resentful that our family and friends are concerned about our mental health.

Some conditions make it hard to seek treatment. This past week, I was in bed with a terrible fever and cold. I didn't know if it was the flu, COVID-19, or bronchitis, but the worse it got, the more I talked myself out of going to see the doctor. I did not want to get dressed and go into the cold air to drive there. Imagine this feeling of being unwell for someone who is suffering from depression. Making an appointment and even getting on a Zoom appointment felt like an impossible task.

These last examples are societal and cultural issues that typically tend to influence why we pretend to be okay when we're not okay in our homes and workplaces. Many of our family members on both sides have not acknowledged the significant mental health crisis I have experienced. Why? Because I don't attend church. Both sides of our families are deeply rooted in the Christian faith. As I shared my journey with them, my diagnosis has been blamed on my lack of connection with God, or I've been told prayer will make it go away. I won't get into my religious ideology here, and I certainly won't dismiss the power of prayer. Still, I have never, ever heard of anyone with cancer being told that they got cancer because they didn't pray hard enough or that they should pray instead of going through chemotherapy.

The final reason I want to explore is that many of us feel we don't have the "right" to feel mentally unwell. Let me give you an example. This past Thanksgiving, I wrote a post on LinkedIn that although I was celebrating the holiday with my husband and daughter, I felt lonely. After my mental health crisis, I have been disconnected from many family members including my mother who has remained estranged since my release from the MHB. Thanksgiving was traditionally a sacred time for our family to spend together, and I missed that time. To my surprise, my post was met with mean comments from readers telling me I didn't have the right to feel lonely because at least I had a husband and child at home. Some people don't have that, so why was I complaining?

Being a Black woman who has enjoyed a successful career, a great marriage, two amazing kids, and a sizeable income, I've often chastised myself with the same comment, "I don't have the right to be lonely, sad, angry, upset, or depressed. It is a privilege to have had the opportunities I have been granted in life. I should be grateful." I am not alone in this thought process. As I climbed the corporate ladder, I quickly learned that being Black and being perceived as "weak" wouldn't cut it. I was told by one of my first Black women mentors in my first corporate job right out of law school, "Never let them see you cry." And from then on, I didn't.

When we are functioning on the orange and red parts of the mental health spectrum and trying to sell those on the outside that everything is green, we do a disservice to our well-being. It's okay to think positively. We are strong. We are resilient. We are unbreakable. That is good but it's a band-aid, not a long-term strategy to gain understanding. Some have even coined this phenomenon of feeling red on the outside but looking green on the inside as "high-functioning depression" as I mentioned was the case for Cheslie Kryst according to her mother. High-functioning depression isn't a medical term, but rather an attempt to describe a clinically depressed person as functioning because they are working, social, and appear to be navigating through society emotionally well. But this functioning, which is also not functioning, is not just reserved for the clinically depressed, but for other mental health issues that are being masked as well. And this masking isn't self-imposed. For many, especially Black women and people from other marginalized groups, it's required to maintain your career. You have no choice but to fake it till you make it. Or break.

While I was attending law school in Arkansas, my husband applied for a World History teaching position in the school district where we lived. He did not get the teaching job, rather he was offered a "credit recovery" position. This position did not require a teaching degree as the person in this position simply monitors kids who would come into a computer lab and catch up on credits they had previously missed so they could graduate on time. Getting a teaching position in that school district was competitive, so he was grateful to have one foot in the door with the hopes of getting a real teaching job the following year.

After he was hired for the credit recovery job, he found out that a White man without a teaching certification or teaching experience had been hired for the teaching position my husband had initially applied for. Not only did my husband have a teaching certification, but he had nearly five years of teaching experience at that point. While we found this snub pretty messed up, we didn't make a big deal about it. My husband didn't file a complaint or a lawsuit, although he was well within his rights. Well, the person that got hired instead of my husband ended up getting terminated for reasons I won't disclose, and my husband ended up getting the teaching job in the end. Yahoo!

The celebration came too quickly. It was evident after my husband was hired that the principal did not want to hire him, but this time around he had no excuse not to. So, what was this man's next strategy? Bully his new employee out. My dear husband is one of the most committed, dedicated, and engaging teachers I've ever known. He loved the work he did and loved his students, and they loved him back. If he missed a day of school, his students would chastise him for being out, if even for a day, because they adored him so much. Instead of the principal marveling over my husband's rapport with his students (and his incredible teaching skills), the man continued to demonstrate that he did not want him at that school. Did I mention that my husband was the only Black teacher besides the basketball coach? My husband noticed that the principal seemed to treat him differently than his colleagues increasingly. The principal even started to have the other teachers "spy" on my husband and have them report to him if my husband was late to work or if there seemed to be too much laughter coming from his classroom. My husband would observe the principal laughing and talking with the other teachers, but when my husband attempted to engage him, he was shrugged off. Despite any attempts to connect with his boss, it just didn't happen.

Throughout the next couple of years, things continued to escalate. There was nothing my husband could do to be valued by the principal or avoid this man's bullying. After I graduated from law school, I became pregnant with our third child. When I was about twenty weeks pregnant, I passed out at work. My job called my husband's school to inform him that I was being taken to the hospital by ambulance. The principal carried the message up to my husband personally. My husband informed him that I was pregnant and rushed to meet me at the hospital. At the hospital, we discovered our baby did not have a heartbeat. I was scheduled to return to the hospital a couple of days later to give birth to our deceased child. My husband informed his boss of the news and told him that he would return to work in a couple of days.

The next day, my husband received a call from his principal. When we saw his name show up on the caller ID, we thought he was calling to check in on us, but nothing could have been further from the truth. He was calling to ask my husband if he had returned a message from a parent that was given to my husband just minutes before he received the message from my job and rushed out. When my husband informed him that he had not had the opportunity to return the call just yet, the principal replied, "The next time I ask you to do something, only divine intervention should stop you from doing it!" But it was divine intervention that stopped my husband from returning that call. It was the sudden loss of our unborn child.

From that point on, my husband began to experience chest pains when he worked. Twice he asked me to drive him straight to the emergency room after school because he thought he was having a heart attack. But every time they hooked him up to the EKG machine, everything appeared normal. Eventually, we learned that he was experiencing panic attacks. Those attacks started to manifest in other ways as well. Anxiety then turned into depression. I would see my husband spend entire weekends in our dark basement, just lying in our guest bed. The once vibrant teacher that genuinely had a passion for teaching was no more. As the days passed, so did his desire to teach. Ultimately, we decided that it was best that he resigned. He never took a step back into the classroom again.

For five years, my husband endured hostility from his boss. He didn't complain when he was overlooked for a position in favor of a non-qualified person and continued to remain silent as he suffered mental and emotional abuse. Although the mental symptoms began to develop into physical ones, he continued to show up to work every single day without fail. Internally, he was functioning in the red, but outwardly he was green. He never let his students, colleagues, and often even me, know the weight his job was putting on him. Although he was prescribed medication for his anxiety, he never received therapy for healing, and because of that, he has never fully recovered.

I spoke with Licensed Professional Counselor Kimberly Leichty who told me, "While medication can be an important part of an individual's treatment plan, medication alone will not cure or heal the deep wounds caused by prolonged exposure to stress or trauma. If those deep wounds are not healed from the inside out through therapy and trauma-informed care, those wounds will fester and grow until all aspects of life are negatively impacted." Faking it till we make it is not an adequate strategy for overcoming our mental health challenges, whether we have been diagnosed with a mental health disorder or are just experiencing an episodic struggle with our mental health. Not only do we run the risk of experiencing post-traumatic stress, as in the case of my husband, but there are other long-term implications of not properly treating mental health issues.

Faking it leads to feelings of stress, anxiety, and burnout. More than that, keeping up the façade drains us of the precious resources we need to restore our mental health. As we spiral downward, our sense of guilt and shame compounds. We're sad about how we've hidden our sadness, which only makes us sadder. And the even sadder fact is that, if we don't get honest about trying to fake our way through life, we're never going to make it. We won't miraculously flip from red to green. When we finally realize that it's ok to not be ok, we can drop the act. It's only when we stop faking it that we can get on the path to making it.

CHAPTER 6

A SAFE PLACE TO WORK

Each year, publications like *Fortune* publish their top ten companies to work for. In 2012, employees of those organizations were surveyed on factors such as attitudes about the management's credibility, job satisfaction, camaraderie, pay and benefit programs, hiring, communication, and diversity. A decade later, in 2022, there was a shift. New factors were considered, such as whether the employer was prioritizing employee well-being, and fostering cultures of inclusion, purpose, listening, caring, and empathy. As we dawn upon a new age at work, it is clear that to be a great place to work, it must be a *safe* place to work.

I remember the first time an employee at a former company told me they didn't feel safe. The first thing that came to my head was that they felt like they were in some physical danger. As the employee began to talk, it became apparent that she wasn't in any physical danger. She didn't feel *psychologically* safe. There are plenty of academic definitions for what it means to be psychologically safe at work. For me, it's plain and simple. To be psychologically safe means I can show up, speak up, and do my job, and in exchange, I can work in a healthy work environment that is free from negativity, and toxicity, and where I have a sense of belonging and inclusion in addition to my paycheck.

Even as the Head of HR for several organizations throughout my career, there were a few times when I felt psychologically unsafe at work. Being an HR leader gave me a first-hand view of the unfair treatment many employees face at work. Too often, I've had to deliver the unexpected news to someone that their time at an organization has ended due to no fault of their own. Many times, this news has been delivered to the victim of misconduct rather than their aggressor. When I hear people say they don't trust HR, I get it. We, as HR personnel, try our best to follow laws, and policies and do what's right for our employees, but too often, we are fighting a losing battle. In most organizations, it's not about what's right. It's about who's right.

Who doesn't make too much noise?
Who looks the part?
Who plays the part?
Who's bringing in the big bucks?
Who shares the same "values"?

Those values aren't necessarily what's written on the company's website or what they told you at orientation. They are shared judgments about what is important at that point in time, and that won't always include you or your well-being.

Meet Pam.

Pam worked for a big consulting firm that had received many accolades for workplace culture for ten years. She absolutely loved the work she did and the organization. The firm allowed her to fulfill both her personal and professional goals. "I had my baby while working there and received my first promotion while working there." She was a star employee and saw herself retiring from the firm. However, when Pam went on maternity leave, things began to change. Her boss informed her that he had too many direct reports and would be hiring someone else to whom

Pam would report upon her return. Pam met with her new boss while on maternity leave and was excited to be working with her.

Once Pam returned from leave, red flags began to fly almost immediately. Her new boss began asking her questions like, [if you're so good at your job] "why weren't you promoted to this position?" and increased her workload significantly for the next eighteen months. Pam's stress grew significantly to a level where she was soon unable to produce milk for her baby. Then things began to worsen. Pam started to be excluded from important meetings and was kept in the dark about important information. Although she was working long into the wee hours of the morning, her manager would tell her she wasn't working hard enough and was told that "her next review was riding on her working harder."

Physical symptoms started to manifest with the increased pressure from her new boss. She started to feel chest pains, experienced anxiety attacks and became depressed, yet she was still being pressured at work to be the "fun" one as well. At that time, she didn't know about mental health and how much she was struggling. However, each morning as she waited for the train to work, she would fantasize about jumping in front of it. In her head, this was her only way out of walking into her horrible work environment. Luckily, she didn't do that, but she scheduled surgery to get some time off from the pressure at work instead.

After returning from her surgery, she was feeling better and rested, but she returned to the same work conditions and tanked fast. She found herself unable to function at all. After consulting with a mentor, she was advised to reach out to EAP (Employee Assistance Program), but she didn't find the EAP service helpful. Then she was on her own trying to find a mental health provider, which added to her feeling of helplessness and decline. She finally found someone that put her on a month's leave after being diagnosed with severe anxiety and clinical depression. She began to improve slowly, yet her medical leave was about to expire. Unlike medical leave, mental health conditions don't expire. Her doctor also informed her that even if she did return to work, her work conditions would likely not improve, so she decided to quit.

Pam's story sounds similar to when my leadership changed after I was discharged from the mental health facility. It only takes one small change to a work environment to go from career bliss to career diss. It can happen with not only a change of leadership, but with the hiring of a snarky new coworker, a change in responsibilities, or being asked to return to the office after two-plus years of working remotely. When this happens, your whole world is turned upside down. You are left hopeless, helpless, and clueless about what to do next. In many cases, your options are limited. For example, it isn't illegal to be a bad boss in the United States. Even bullying in the workplace is legal as long as you're not singling someone out because of their protected class (their race, gender, age, national origin, etc.). With HR having limited authority over what they can do to protect you and with no legal recourse, there are usually two things left for you to do. Continue to work in an unhealthy work environment or find a new job. Pam reluctantly did the latter. Her dreams of retiring from her firm were dashed. She went from having a great place to work to looking for a safe place to work.

Because most of us have experienced what Pam did, we are reluctant to invest 100% of ourselves in our workplaces. By the time I had my third job out of college, I had learned that I needed to plot my exit strategy from the day I was hired. I know you're probably wondering what that exit strategy looked like, right? I'll speak more about this later in the book, but here's a glimpse. Every day, I would spend a few minutes scouring open positions that I was qualified for or almost qualified for. I wouldn't apply for the positions, but I wanted to keep abreast of what organizations were looking for in my field. Was there some new certification that I needed to get? A new competency? I wanted to ensure my resume was always in the most tip, top shape. I also documented everything: conversations, accomplishments, performance reviews, and other people's promotions. EVERYTHING. Next, I always worked a second job. I've been an adjunct professor at several colleges and universities for over a decade. In the instances that the next day would unexpectedly be my final day at an organization, I had a small income to fall back on. And, finally, I was building my own business on the side. As you can see, planning your exit strategy while working full-time is like working two full-time jobs. It's exhausting and should be unnecessary, but it is very needed.

Take, for instance, Twitter. I know many employees who worked at Twitter and were proud of their work. However, after Elon Musk bought out Twitter, their days of working at the tech company ended abruptly with no regard for civility, compassion, or appreciation for the people who had propelled the company's success. One laid-off employee was eight months pregnant and had a nine-month-old and instead of receiving a phone call from her boss or HR informing her of her status, her laptop access was abruptly cut off. Thousands of others had their access to their laptops and emails cut off before being formally informed that their jobs were being eliminated.

For those who weren't impacted, a second gut punch was thrown. All remaining employees were called back to the office on a full-time basis. Remote work had permanently come to an end, although Twitter employees had been informed that remote work would be permanent. To add to that, Musk called for the remaining employees to work "long hours with high intensity." To help them with this, he also eliminated "rest days" that were previously implemented to promote mental and physical well-being.

What we're witnessing was the end of an era where for a brief period in history, employees were able to call the shots. Due to the outcome of the great resignation, where a record number of employees refused to return to toxic, unhealthy work environments, employees were able to demand more flexibility, better pay, and enhanced benefits. However, with the economy shifting, so does the power. Layoffs in the once-secure tech sector are taking place by the day. As interest rates rise and inflation increases, employees no longer feel comfortable leaving their jobs. With power being handed back to workplaces, the mental well-being of every worker is at risk. While Musk's disregard for the mental well-being of Twitter employees is overt and brash, he is not alone. Other organizations have subtly reverted to the harsh, intense work climates we experienced before the COVID-19 pandemic. The glimpse of kindness, humanity, and compassion that were demonstrated during the COVID-19 pandemic are fading away. For the past two years, organizational leaders invited their employees into conversations about dismantling the systems and structures that proved to be obstacles to working in healthy, positive, and psychologically safe work environments. Now, they appear to be rebuilding those barriers, brick by brick, wall by wall.

Have you ever tried to open a website and received a message that you couldn't access that page or some of its content due to a firewall? According to Checkpoint, a cyber security software company, "A firewall is a network security device that monitors and filters incoming and outgoing network traffic based on an organization's previously established security policies. At its most basic, a firewall is essentially the barrier between a private internal network and the public internet. A firewall's main purpose is to allow non-threatening traffic in and to keep dangerous traffic out."[11]

The moment an employee shares that they have been diagnosed with a mental health disorder or are struggling with their mental health, a big firewall goes up. Red lights start flashing. You are now a danger and a threat. Organizations define "dangerous"

---

[11] What is a Firewall?, CheckPoint, https://www.checkpoint.com/cyber-hub/network-security/what-is-firewall/#:~:text=A%20Firewall%20is%20a%20network,network%20and%20the%20public%20Interne, accessed March 15, 2023.

employees differently than in the traditional sense of the word. A "dangerous" employee can cause harm, threat, or discomfort to the organization by becoming a legal risk or engaging in what they think is disruptive behavior. When I returned to my executive position at the MHA, I didn't know it, but firewalls went up all around me. Now that I had been diagnosed with a mental health condition, I was no longer perceived as competent so my position needed to be "supplemented" with another person. Perhaps because of my legal background, it was feared that I would be litigious, so my manager refused to speak with me one-on-one. My every effort to show that I was still capable, competent, and ready to contribute the same value I had before my diagnosis was seen as dangerous or some sort of threat, and a firewall would pop up.

Disabling a firewall on the internet is pretty straightforward (although you'll get plenty of messages advising you not to do so), but it's not as easy in the workplace. It's a long, intentional process that requires education, training, perspective-shifting, and dismantling. I'm not a tech person, so I'll stop with the IT references here, but the next time you try to access a website, and a firewall won't allow you, I want you to remember that moment. Think how frustrating it was for you not to be able to access something that you desired. Some firewall error messages only give you the option to "return back to safety," leaving you wondering what threat ever existed. Instead of putting firewalls in place to block people with mental health struggles out of the workplace, organizations should be blocking the attitudes, biases, prejudices, policies, and systems that contribute to poor mental health.

I've spoken to and read the stories of thousands of people who have experienced a mental health struggle, and an overwhelming majority of them stated that they had not struggled with their mental health until a workplace-related incident occurred. Why is it that the very place that many of us solely rely on for mental health resources such as medical and prescription benefits, employee assistance programs, and other resources are the very places that make us need them? The recent acknowledgment that organizations must do better at promoting the mental health of their workforces has been promising. Organizations recognize Mental Health Awareness Month, and World Mental Health Day, offering mental health breaks, and more access to mental health providers. Society's perception of mental illness is slowly shifting as well. The fact that a wildly popular TV show like *Ted Lasso* could build an entire season around its main character's crippling anxiety is a sign that the world is ready to discuss and deal with mental illness the same way we would any other disease—without all of the shame and stigma.

This is all excellent news, but for business leaders and their workforces, cultivating cultures of mental wellness in the workplace is very new and challenging to navigate. What does effective support look like for someone who has been informed that they're struggling with their mental health? How do I set boundaries for myself to prevent burnout? How do I ask for reasonable accommodations without looking like I'm not committed to my work? These are the questions that the next part of this book will address. Cultivating cultures of mental wellness in the workplace is more than writing up a few new policies, giving access to apps, and bringing in a yoga instructor. Not one story I've shared with you yet mentioned any of those things. It's about developing a culture of comprehensive inclusion. Whether someone is struggling with their mental health or not, workplaces should be proactive at providing comprehensive mental wellness solutions, with the biggest solution being a culture shift. It takes a cultural commitment to wellness that fosters *every* employee's social, emotional, and spiritual health in the workplace.

But there's something else I am compelled to share: protecting your mental health is your responsibility, not your job's. That might sound counterintuitive to everything I've written in this book. It's nice to have workplaces that provide you with support, resources, medical insurance, empathy, compassion, and kindness, but when it comes to your health, whether physical or mental, it's on you. Oftentimes we wait on the circumstances around us to magically change for us to feel better.

"Maybe one day soon, my organization will see what a jerk my boss is and get rid of him."

"Perhaps they will realize that laying off that person on my team wasn't such a good idea after all because they'll see that those of us who have remained are stretched beyond our limits."

"Surely there will be a job opening soon for the work I really want to do because I'm not really finding my purpose in what I'm doing now."

These things, thoughts, and perceptions—realities—won't magically go away, and we must be purposeful and intentional with the people, circumstances, and environments that we invite into our lives. We've all been guilty of *passively* addressing our mental health or not taking care of our mental health at all. We sometimes don't even acknowledge that our brain is an essential organ until something goes wrong with it. My entire life, I've been consistent with going for my annual dental, visual, and GYN exams. It wasn't until I was diagnosed with a mental health condition that I began to consistently check on my mental health. Not only do I receive regular treatment from a licensed mental health provider, but there are additional measures I take to protect my mental health just like I do my physical health. And because I now know how much my professional life impacts my mental well-being (and yours, too!), I pay close attention to workplace triggers and boundaries that may cause mental and emotional harm.

Those of us who have a diagnosed mental health condition deserve and should be allowed the opportunity to contribute our knowledge and talents to workplaces without the fear of those firewalls going up trying to block us out. Just like those with physical and visible disabilities, our work should be accessible and designed for our unique talents and capabilities.

For the next part of this book, I've interviewed some of the most acclaimed mental health professionals from around the world, read the latest evidence-based research, and tapped into my employment law expertise, and my time as an HR executive. What I've learned as someone living with a mental health condition is that part of the solution is to provide people struggling with tools, resources, and guidance for going from being burned out, unhappy, and unmotivated to reclaiming their mental health at work.

If you're an organization or organizational leader, don't worry, I've got you covered too. After reading this book, your workforce can feel empowered to ignite a movement toward healthier and safer work environments. As a leader, you will play a significant role in this movement. Don't look at this as "something else to add to your plate." Look at it as an investment in your most valuable asset- your people. And let's not forget, leaders are people too. Mental health knows no titles, paychecks, or organizational hierarchy. I experienced my mental health crisis while working in the c-suite. So, let's work collectively to ensure everyone has a great and safe workplace.

PART III

Crazy

&

FORGING
AHEAD

"

Martin Luther King is well known for his unrelenting fight for the civil rights of Black people in the United States. What is less known, however, was his silent struggle with mental health. As a child, King twice attempted suicide. Later in life, he survived an assassination attempt, spent countless nights in jail, and constantly received threats to his life. Before his assassination, it is reported that he struggled immensely with his mental health and his staff had tried to secure a psychiatric intervention. Still, he held to his convictions of making life better for his kids and mine. Although he would eventually reckon with his imminent mortality, he never ceased to abandon his mission. He forged ahead, fighting for equality until his dying day.

CHAPTER 7

DREAMING THE
IMPOSSIBLE DREAM

"To dream the impossible dream
To fight the unbeatable foe
To bear with unbearable sorrow
To run where the brave dare not go…"

These are lyrics from the song "The Impossible Dream" from the musical, *Man of La Mancha*, which is based on the book, *Don Quixote*. My mother was a music teacher, so we often listened to musical soundtracks as children. Whenever I listened to this song, something resonated with me. I would be struck with this sudden unexplainable strength that I believed could conquer anything. This song inspired a tagline on my consulting firm's website: "Helping Organizations Conquer the Impossible. Achieve the Unthinkable." Some organizations may believe that I was referring to my services as helping them to achieve astonishing financial profits or some other big audacious goal of theirs, but that wasn't what I had in mind. I wanted to help organizations create healthy work environments where the employee's career dreams didn't end in nightmares.

Even before becoming a mental health advocate, I had witnessed firsthand and had been a victim of toxic, unhealthy, uncompassionate, uncivil, and disrespectful workplaces. It upset me to watch budding new employees who had either just graduated from college, transitioned careers, or had just received a job offer after getting uncountable rejections go from smiling and jumping for joy for their new opportunity to barely being able to put one foot in front of the other when walking into their workplace. I remember when my husband finally got that teaching job that he had initially been rejected from and how he didn't tell me he had gotten the job. Instead, he tricked me into believing that we were going to his workplace for one thing, but the next thing I knew, he was putting a key into the lock of his new classroom. My eyes watered as I met his eyes, and we both hugged and jumped for joy. That key to his new classroom, which meant a new job, was like getting the key to a brand-new Aston Martin. It wasn't the $50,000.00 salary we were excited about (although we sure needed it at that point as I was still in law school). It was the fact that we knew he was a phenomenal teacher from whom every high school kid deserved to learn. We excitedly decorated his room and got everything ready for his first day. He then spent the remainder of his available time before the first day of school meticulously preparing his lesson plans. His students would get a world-class learning experience! But you already know how that story ended. He didn't quit teaching ten years later because the students were more eager to learn than he was to teach. Or because of uncooperative parents. Or because he was being paid crumbs for someone with his amount of college education and experience. He exited his entire career and didn't look back because of one person's behavior. The principal's, that is. His boss.

Well, I take that back. It wasn't exclusively due to the actions and behavior of one person. It was a systemic issue. My husband did inform the leaders at the district level about the way he was being treated, and they did nothing. Are you surprised? In their eyes, this school was one of the top-ranked in the country. It also excelled in sports and other extracurricular activities. The district leaders could've cared less that this Black teacher was having a bad work experience there. As far as they were concerned, the principal was a high performer and made the school district look good. If my husband wanted to leave, he could very well go and teach at another school. That was their first suggestion. They even tried to convince him that he was making the stories up in his head, which worsened his mental health. We tried everything to convince the school district that my husband was mistreated due to his race, but no one would listen. Eventually, we filed a complaint with the Equal Employment Opportunity Commission (E.E.O.C.), and ironically, once word got out about his racial discrimination charge in the school district, the other few Black teachers in the school district came to us privately to share their similar experiences. We pleaded with them to join us in our fight for justice, but they were too fearful of what would happen to their jobs. We were in this fight alone. While we received a nominal monetary settlement, we lost the battle. Our goal wasn't money, after all. Our goal was to unmask the systemic racism that existed in this historically White school district. To have the system administrators acknowledge that it was a problem. To get rid of the problem. And, most importantly, for my husband to be able to teach in a healthy work environment where he could focus on his number one priority: his students.

We didn't know it then, but we were "dream[ing] the impossible dream." *Fighting the unbeatable foe.* We were having to *bear with unbearable sorrow.* But we *ran where the brave dare not go.* Let's unpack that last line. "We ran where the brave dare not go." I have encountered plenty of people who are among the bravest, most courageous, boldest people I know, but when it came to going against "the Man," uhm, hum, our workplaces, even some of the bravest dare not go. Why? Because it's likely a losing battle. Sometimes, the bravest thing to do is to walk away. Walk away from that dream that you wanted for so long. That salary puts food on the table, and that insurance covers your medical needs. As I think about it, one of the bravest things you can do is to walk away from a battle you can't win and, instead, put your mental well-being first.
Based on the stories I've shared in Parts I and II of this book, walking away is the only solution to putting your mental health first. I've shared with you my experience walking away (or being

escorted away). But, as I reflect on it now, working in a healthy, positive work environment isn't dreaming an impossible dream. I've experienced it! Remember, I told you that before my mental health crisis, I was happily employed as the Chief Human Resources Officer at a mental health hospital? I was happy, motivated, valued, seen, heard, and felt psychologically safe for four years. There were two reasons I could achieve this level of work bliss: I was passionate and committed to the work that I did, had a leader that saw my passion, commitment, and value. He also ensured that there were no barriers for me to use my knowledge, expertise, and experience to remove systemic barriers to equity, address unconscious bias, and identify threats to healthy work culture. Ironically, when I began my role, I didn't think it would work out the way it had. I went straight into planning my exit strategy. But, over time, things slowly changed, not just for me but for everyone working at the hospital. Even our relationship with the union leaders changed from adversarial to collaborative. My experience of actually working in a healthy and positive work environment firsthand gives me hope that others can experience this too. And as the Head of H.R., I had the privilege of knowing firsthand of how culture can be transformed from being on the verge of being toxic to one that is nourishing and in which people could thrive. In Part III of this book, I will provide a pathway in which organizational leaders and their workforce individuals can identify and remove the systemic barriers that are blocking access to healthy and psychologically safe workplaces. They can also work together to cultivate cultures of mental wellness that include preventing burnout and finding happiness and motivation at work.

Cultivating mental wellness in the workplace is a two-way street. I will provide the strategies for those in both positional authority and individual contributors. So, it's up to you AND your workplace. I emphasize this point because some people work in careers where they have found purpose and passion and genuinely want to succeed. Then there are those who, *regardless* of what their organization does, will not be happy at work and dread going there. Every. Single. Day. Before attending law school, I spent countless years working in department stores for extra money. I was miserable. I worked these jobs in addition to my full-time jobs which meant working nights, weekends, and most holidays. I also had to stand on my feet for long periods of time. And did I mention that I worked in the shoe department? Fighting toddlers to size their feet and dealing with indecisive parents wasn't my cup of tea. We won't even talk about the madness of the Annual Easy Spirit Sale (that was for your 65 and over crowd). I hated it, and they could have paid me a million dollars a year, rolled out the red carpet every time I stepped in the door, and assigned Mother Theresa as my manager, and I still would have found something to complain about. But, to my surprise, some people had been working in those shoe departments for years, planned on retiring from those department stores, and loved their jobs. Their faces lit up every time someone walked into the department because they couldn't wait to fit them with a brand-new pair of shoes! I didn't get it. But, later on, I did. Not EVERY job is fit for everybody but there is A job for everybody. I say all of that to reinforce that if you are in the wrong job or career, no book can help with that. But, if you're dealing with a toxic work environment, bad leadership, unsupportive coworkers, and pay equity issues but enjoy doing your actual job, these two parts of the book are for you!

Let's return to my four years of bliss as the Chief Human Resources Officer at a mental health hospital. As already mentioned, it wasn't always the perfect work environment. I had just been terminated because of the jury duty fiasco and didn't think I'd ever work again, but now was the time to start afresh. This opportunity was my first and only c-suite position, and I was super excited. On my first day, a biweekly department head meeting was being held. So that meant that I would be introduced to all of the business partners I would be supporting from an H.R. standpoint. When I walked into the meeting, I was ready for this new, exciting opportunity for my career. At a long conference table, my new boss, the C.E.O. of the hospital, sat with about twenty people, and several other people were seated in chairs along the wall. My new boss signaled for me to take a seat at an empty chair beside him and I gladly sat down and made eye contact with as many people as possible to give my new colleagues a smile and nod. Then something unexpected happened that changed the trajectory of my entire morning and my perspective of how I would spend my time there. Before the meeting even began, my new boss leaned over and whispered, "What's your last name?"

I was devastated to hear him ask this as I believed that he was just as excited about me starting this position as I was. Wouldn't he then have memorized my name? My dreams were crushed. Why was I there? Did they desperately need someone in this position and quickly hired me? Was I a *diversity* hire? I went from being the most confident, excited person in the room to the most invisible. That beaming smile faded as I quietly whispered back, "Bowman." I wanted to continue with, "And, don't you ever forget it" but stopped myself. He then read my bio from a piece of paper to the attendees. It was like we had never met. I felt like I was just a temp sent in from an agency that would be there only briefly.

I would soon find out I was right. My boss did think I would be there only briefly. His experience with the previous H.R. leaders could have gone better, certainly. I would later find the H.R. department in a hot mess. For one, there was no Human Resources Information System (H.R.I.S.) system. An H.R.I.S. is a system that tracks employee movement, such as when they were fired, separated, promoted, had a pay increase, etc. The broken-down system being used at the mental health hospital still had deceased and terminated employees as active. So that meant that whenever we ran an all-employee report, it had almost every single employee that had ever worked there for the past sixty years, and we had to remove them manually. I had my work cut out for me and not just for building an H.R. infrastructure but also to gain the trust and respect of my peers in the c-suite. H.R. had not been a valuable source for them, and something had to change.

Here's the thing. It took me only a short time to turn that department around. It wasn't because of my superpower, i.e., H.R. expertise. It was because of some very pertinent factors:

 Despite not knowing my last name on that first day, my C.E.O. always treated me with respect and didn't micromanage or put pressure on me to get everything turned around in an unreasonable amount of time. And, most importantly, he provided me with the resources I needed when I requested them.

 Even though my peers and business partners had yet to get the best results from working with the H.R. department in the past, they took a chance and partnered with me.

 The H.R. team had much to learn but was willing and eager to do so. They hadn't been developed at all and were thirsting for it. Those unwilling to learn and/or do things differently were asked to leave. I could quickly tell who those people were and didn't waste their time or mine by keeping them around for a long time. As a side note, terminating someone who doesn't have the potential to meet the expectations of a job can sometimes be the most respectful thing you can do for that person, especially if done the right way.

 The labor union soon learned we had the same goal: to give their members a warm, welcoming, positive, and inclusive workplace. I was willing to admit when we (the hospital) had made the wrong decision about an employment matter. And, in contrast, if I thought we had made the right decision, I articulated that position in a thoughtful, respectful manner.

I could go on and on about how the H.R. function was able to go from being a department that needed to be more trusted and practical to being a well-respected and relied-upon business function. But that's not my point here. The point is that I had walked into some of the worst conditions a new hire could enter. However, those conditions had nothing to do with the work culture or environment and that made all the difference in the world.

Some would have thought I was crazy for staying in that job once I realized how much work needed to be done (which wasn't shared with me during the job interview), but I don't think any of us should be scared of a challenge. We do, however, need the right working conditions to protect our mental health. There were times when my mental health was being compromised, and not because of my bipolar disorder; instead, it was being triggered by workplace stressors. Those first couple of months working there were challenging and made me feel burned out. But, after those first couple of months, with the support of a leader that I had admired and a positive work culture, I was able to avoid being burned out, unmotivated, and unhappy and maintain my mental health. This allowed me to forge ahead to accomplish achievements that I am to this day exceptionally proud of.

For the remaining part of this section, I will provide a framework for how I protected my mental health at work despite working in high-paced, stressed-out, non-ideal conditions and what my employer did to provide me with a safe place to achieve this. I will also lean into what I could have done differently when I let my workplace get the best of me. To complement my experience, I will also share the stories of those who too have maintained their mental health at work. And, of course, you will be hearing advice from some of the most acclaimed mental health experts from across the globe. I am so excited about writing these last two parts because the first two, in some respect, were pretty grim. I will admit that. But no matter how seemingly bleak they were, the stories of those who have struggled with their mental health and were not treated fairly deserved to be shared. I aim to share fewer stories about those who were treated unfairly due to their mental health conditions in the future and share more stories about those who were able to thrive at work despite their mental health.

Anything is possible if your workplace is healthy and psychologically safe, even an impossible dream. So, let's get to making those once-unachievable dreams come true.

Without further ado, I want to introduce you to:

THE
RECLAIM YOUR F.A.M.E. AT WORK
FRAMEWORK

I named this framework Reclaim Your F.A.M.E. because I found a common theme among the workplace mental health stories I had heard, including my own. That theme was people plummeting from *rockstar status* to *rock bottom* in a short span of time. You see, many people begin their jobs by "hitting the ground running." They excel, exceed expectations, have excellent interpersonal relationships, and love their work. Then something changes that dynamic. These changes are the variables that I have written about previously: people, places, or things. After any of these variables change, that is when the shift or shit happens. Is it possible to get your rockstar status back after that shift? Can your star shine again? Can you reclaim your fame? I believe you can when you are provided with adequate resources and support from your employer. The F.A.M.E. framework is an easy-to-follow guide for employees and employers to cultivate cultures of mental wellness in the workplace. If organizational leaders and individual contributors Foster equity, have Awareness, Manage burnout, and Exit harm. Then, guess what? Mental wellness follows.

Yes, I transformed fame into an acronym because acronyms are just easier to follow, understand, and remember. The F.A.M.E. acronym will guide us through the framework from burned out, unhappy, and unmotivated to reclaiming our mental health at work. Even if you're not burned out, unhappy, or unmotivated or have yet to start your job, you can use this framework once you enter the workplace. F.A.M.E. also serves as a guide for organizational leaders. The truth is in the pudding. Your organization is going nowhere if it doesn't promote the mental well-being of its workforce. Your organization will likely experience high turnover, low productivity, and underutilization of untapped value and talent. But you already know that, don't you? Or maybe you just need a quick reminder. In the process of writing this book, over 40,000 jobs were eliminated in the once highly sought-after tech industry over the course of one week. Surely, organizations can use a little guidance on reclaiming their FAME as well. With that, let's get to it!

CHAPTER 8

FOSTERING EQUITY

My husband and I are big boxing fans. My husband enjoys the physical athleticism of the sport. I am more intrigued that boxing entails something more prevalent than any other sport that I've watched. If you're unfamiliar with boxing, one thing to note is that a lot happens leading up to a fight. There is a lot of preparation and training for the boxers, press conferences, and in-depth analysis of their opponent to determine who is more likely to emerge as the big winner and why. Even before agreeing to enter a match, each boxer has a ton of information about their opponent to know if the fight will be an equitable matchup. This information is very transparent. They know their opponent's height, weight, arms reach, whether they are left or right-handed, and who their trainers are. How many fights have they won or lost? In what rounds? Did they win by knockout or by the decision? When was their last fight? What are their tendencies, weaknesses, and strengths? Then, there are the rules by the Boxing Commission. First, there are weight classes. For instance, a boxer weighing 200 pounds would never fight someone weighing 140 pounds. Each fighter must weigh in before the day of the fight to ensure they still fall into their weight class. Additionally, each fighter undergoes testing to ensure that they have not taken any performance-enhancing drugs, which would give them an unearned and unfair advantage. But what I enjoy most is what happens once the opponents are in the ring. There the referee plays a significant role. The referee ensures that there are no hits below the belt, head-butting, or rabbit punching (which is a blow to the back of the head that can cause severe brain and spinal injury). Additionally, the referee can stop the fight if a boxer is in distress. Because they know that there are millions of spectators watching, the referees rarely make bad calls or miss anything. If you examine the totality of the sport, boxing fosters equity for its participants. Each fighter knows what they face before they step into the ring, and no one has an unearned advantage. If a fighter loses a match, the losing fighter concedes that the other fighter had an *earned* advantage. Imagine if your workplace operated in this same manner.

Unlike boxers, we often enter our workplaces without true transparency of the environment. We are fighting "heavyweights" – people, structures, and systems far outside our "weight class." We also don't have a referee ensuring we are not "hit below the belt, head-butted, or rabbit-punched, or telling us to call it quits if we're in distress. Additionally, no eyes are watching our everyday interactions, guaranteeing the shots are called right or, in other words, demanding accountability. Wouldn't it be great to have someone jump in right when you receive a microaggression and shout out, "Hey, that was below the belt!"

I have already shared countless stories of people who have experienced a mental health crisis or have been diagnosed with a mental health condition while working. As you can see, there is little doubt that when it comes to mental health, there are inequities in how those with mental health conditions are treated as opposed to those with physical health conditions. As a former H.R. leader, I always urged managers they should never to discuss the disability status of their employees. Why? Because the managers may fall into the trap of using that information to make unconscious discriminatory decisions. Remember how I shared that my former manager treated me differently when I was diagnosed with COVID-19 than after I was diagnosed with bipolar disorder? The differentiation in my treatment was a prime example of inequitable treatment. I have chosen to use the word equity rather than equality because equality means that you treat everyone the same; equity means that, unlike in boxing, we don't all start from a level playing field. Some have unearned advantages; others have unearned disadvantages. Workplaces must acknowledge and rectify these imbalances.

Although managers have traditionally been cautioned against engaging or asking questions about someone's health status, this directive does not apply to every situation. I have said it before, and I will repeat it. If an employee approaches their manager and informs them that they have been diagnosed with cancer, their manager is unlikely to reply with, "I can't discuss this with you. Please speak with Human Resources or call the Employee Assistance Program." Instead, the manager, in all probability, will engage in a thoughtful, compassionate, and empathetic conversation with said employee. They may ask about what stage of cancer the person is facing, their treatment plan, and, more importantly, how they can support them. This is true for most other physical, particularly visible, illnesses as well. A study conducted by Mental Health First Aid (M.H.F.A.) England found that "just 14% of employees felt they could talk about common mental health issues in the workplace, compared to 42% who felt comfortable discussing physical problems."[12] The question is, why is there such a discrepancy between talking about a physical problem and a mental health condition? Why are we less likely to receive the same compassion, empathy, and thoughtful conversation when we are honest about our mental health?

---

[12] Study: Most Employees Not Comfortable Discussing Mental Health At Work, Wellable, June 6, 2022, https://www.wellable.co/blog/most-employees-not-comfortable-discussing-mental-health-at-work/.

The answer is, unlike cancer patients, we will, in most cases, be discriminated against. After my bipolar disorder diagnosis, I pivoted my workplace equity work to workplace mental health advocacy. I wanted to bring awareness to the challenges I faced while navigating the workplace with a mental health condition and find solutions so that others would not have to face the same challenges. With that mission in mind, my husband and I co-founded The Bowman Foundation for Workplace Equity and Mental Wellness (The Bowman Foundation). Our first action was to conduct a survey[13] on the current state of mental health in the workplace. The results showed that while most respondents admitted to struggling with their mental health, disclosing mental health disorders to employers remains an issue. Most of the comments about the current state of mental health in the workplace were related to instances of retaliation or fear of retaliation from employers. Recurring themes included:

- reduced job assignments
- less visibility on projects
- unfavorable performance evaluations due to attendance
- micromanagement after disclosure
- isolation
- termination

One respondent wrote, "After [my] P.T.S.D. was disclosed, I got moved out of my role, and my job was eliminated after 24 years." Interestingly, respondents from marginalized groups were more likely to be retaliated against than non-marginalized groups. You're probably thinking, "See, that's why I would never disclose my mental health condition at work!" I get that! But let's think about that for a minute. To do so, let's shift perspectives. Why do

---

[13] The Bowman Foundation for Workplace Equity & Mental Wellness, https://thebowmanfoundation.org/wp-content/uploads/2022/09/Mental_Health_White_Paper-.pdf, accessed March 20, 2023

people with physical (non-mental) health conditions feel more comfortable disclosing their diagnosis than those with mental health conditions? Here are a few reasons.

Over the past decades, organizations have spent an enormous amount of resources on improving the physical well-being of their employees. Every organization I have ever been employed with has conducted some form of annual steps and weight loss challenge, heart health awareness initiative, and smoking cessation program. However, according to the *Journal of Occupational and Environmental Medicine*, "mental disorders top the list of the most burdensome and costly illnesses in the United States at over $200 billion a year, well exceeding the cost burden of heart disease, stroke, cancer, and obesity."[14] But, until recently, there were little to no mental wellness campaigns or challenges in organizations. The case can be made that physical well-being equates to mental well-being, but that is not always true. Other factors must be considered besides physical health, such as environmental, social, cultural, and genetics. In short, I could be training for a marathon and be in tip-top physical shape, but if my work culture sucks and no one seems to care to do anything about it, my mental health can be negatively impacted. When my husband was dealing with his school principal, he walked five miles daily and ate a balanced diet. His bloodwork was perfect, but due to the treatment he was receiving from his manager, he began to experience anxiety attacks and depression for the first time in his life.

With most wellness programs centered on physical well-being, talking about physical health has become a more common practice among employees. Think about it. You notice that one of your colleagues has lost a lot of weight. You compliment them and may even ask them to share their weight loss strategies. Another

---

[14] Ron Z Goetzel PhD et al, Mental Health in the Workplace: A Call to Action Proceedings From the Mental Health in the Workplace—Public Summit, Journal of Occupational and Environmental Medicine, April 2018, https://journals.lww.com/joem/FullText/2018/04000/Mental_Health_in_t he_Workplace__A_Call_to_Action.5.aspx

colleague shares that they stopped smoking a few months ago. You give them a high five and tell them to keep it up. They may have even received a financial incentive to do so. One of my former organizations gave away trips to Paris to the winning team and their families as the prize for a step challenge! This challenge became so competitive that it was rumored that some of the competitors put their pedometers on their dogs as they ran around their yards! So, with all the compassion, empathy, support, even celebration, and incentives centered around physical health, it is no wonder people feel more comfortable opening up *and* supporting the discussion. I have yet to work for an organization that gives you an incentive for when you are clinically depressed, and everything in your body wants you to stay in bed, your house is a mess, and you have barely taken care of yourself and your kids. Yet, you still make it to work and give it your best, even if your best did not exactly meet expectations.

Even when it comes to mental health conditions, there are inequities in how they are perceived and how people with the conditions are treated. A recent study conducted by Indiana University revealed that for the first time "stigma toward people with depression has dropped significantly" in the United States[15]. However, disappointingly, the study also noted that stigma levels for other mental illnesses remain "stagnant" while stigma around schizophrenia and alcohol dependency has increased. The findings of this research were not shocking to me. On social media, I see more and more people (especially millennials and Gen Z) talking about their struggles with depression, anxiety, and A.D.H.D., but very few people post about their struggles with schizophrenia, bipolar disorder, alcohol, and drug abuse.

---

[15] Stigma surrounding depression drops for first time in U.S., but increases for other mental illnesses, Press Release from News at IU, Indiana University, December 21, 2021, https://news.iu.edu/live/news/27821-stigma-surrounding-depression-drops-for-first-time

While there has been some progress in the perceptions of mental health conditions in the workplace, it goes without saying that stigma is the most significant barrier to an equitable work environment for those struggling with their mental health. Let's examine how these inequities manifest at work:

- **Organizational priorities on physical vs. mental well-being:** I've already covered this one earlier in this chapter, so I won't go any deeper.

- **Medical benefits:** Even though mental health parity is required by law; organizations spend more on physical health expenditures.

- **Access to mental health providers:** Even if an organization provides medical insurance, access to mental health providers remains a barrier. The ratio of mental health providers to the employee population is 9 psychiatrists to every 100,000 Americans. If that statistic is not shocking enough, of the 3,000 counties in the United States, 60% have no local psychiatrist. I won't even go into the lack of diversity among mental health providers that are available, which can negatively impact care (remember how my psychiatrist tried to send me to jail and called C.P.S. because I asked for help?)

- **Performance evaluations:** People with mental health conditions are more often penalized during job evaluations for excessive absences due to their conditions, even when the absences are covered under job-protected leaves. After I was discharged from the mental health facility, I needed additional leave time to find and adjust to medications. The side effects of psychiatric medications can include drowsiness, dizziness, upset stomach, and sweating from top to bottom. Lithium, a medication commonly prescribed to patients with bipolar disorder, made me even forget my name on some days. If I didn't know my name, how was I supposed to know how to do my job? Ironically, many of these side effects are also seen in chemotherapy treatment. However, it is much more acceptable to say you are out on long-term disability for chemo than that you are adjusting to your bipolar meds.

Upward Mobility: If you receive low-performance review ratings due to absences related to your mental health condition, you will likely not get a promotion. If you recall, I had to divide my Head of H.R. job with the person who had been covering for me when I returned from my leave of absence. Before my suicide attempt and subsequent leave, my role had been expanded to assist another hospital with labor negotiations. I was even being stretched to cover some of the operational functions at my facility. My husband, seeing the work I was putting in, even announced one day, "You're on track to becoming a C.E.O. or C.O.O. of one of these hospitals in the future!" I was excited about the potential opportunity for growth. However, as we know, that did not go as planned. Not only were my responsibilities reduced, but I also eventually exited the organization to protect my mental health.

Retaliation: Besides receiving low ratings on job evaluations, people with mental health conditions are far more likely to be retaliated against once the employers know about their condition than those with non-mental health-related conditions.

Pay Inequities: Studies show that people working in the U.S. and the U.K. with serious mental health conditions are paid less than people without serious mental health conditions[16].

---

[16] Nikki Bond, Mind the mental health income gap, Money and Mental Health Policy Institute, September 22, 2020,

Avoidance of Mental Health Care: Because of the institutional, structural stigma associated with mental health conditions, those struggling with their mental health will not obtain the care they need. As I wrote about in Chapter Two, there continue to be unnecessary policies and processes that discourage and even obstruct people from seeking out treatment. One example is when lawyers and doctors are asked about their mental health history as part of the application process for obtaining licenses for their professions. Knowing that this history must be disclosed and afraid that their application may be denied, some avoid getting the treatment they need, potentially worsening their condition. To underscore how important it is to remove or modify this barrier and encourage rather than discourage treatment, a startling statistic posted by *The Washington Post* reveals that one physician takes their life every day, which is twice the rate of the general population[17].

I could go on and on about the inequities that people with mental health conditions face in the workplace, but I'd be remiss if I didn't mention that these inequities are more persistent and prevalent for people in marginalized groups. They are also compounded by other negative experiences in the workplace, as discussed in Parts I and II of this book. Ongoing discriminatory and unjust treatment due to your race, gender, sexuality, ethnicity, and so on adversely impacts your mental health. Inequitable work environments have already oppressed people in marginalized groups, so adding the additional mental health conditions inequities sees harsher results. For instance, Black women are

---

https://www.latimes.com/business/story/2023-02-23/mental-health-and-the-workplace

[17] https://www.washingtonpost.com/outlook/2020/05/11/mental-health-doctors-covid/

leaving Corporate America at an alarming rate to start their own businesses after being exhausted by microaggressions, belittling, and burnout. One woman cited that after experiencing the workplace norms for Black women, "she became agoraphobic, experienced insomnia and anxiety, and reached a breaking point. After 15 months at the company, in September, she quit to become her own boss."[18]

Whether you were struggling with your mental health before you started your job or your work conditions caused your mental health struggles, you will not be on a level playing field with those who are not struggling with their mental health. So, does that mean you are screwed? Are there no opportunities to level the playing field? I know there are. There is always space to create equitable work environments. It takes time, effort, intentionality, and patience. Still, I firmly believe that with the right blueprint, equity in the workplace can be achieved, even for those with mental health conditions.

The question is, how?

For the remainder of this chapter, I will provide a blueprint for the first part of reclaiming your F.A.M.E. in the workplace, beginning with **fostering equity**. Some of you reading this are not in management positions and may believe that you do not have a role in fostering equity at work. I beg to differ. That belief has been a primary barrier. While organizational leaders play a huge role in cultivating equitable work environments, we cannot rely

---

[18] Alexandra York and Marguerite Ward, Black women are worn out from discrimination in corporate America. They're leaving to launch their own businesses, creating a hole for talent across industries., Business Insider magazine, February 6, 2023, https://www.businessinsider.com/black-women-leaving-corporate-america-entreprenurship-startups-2022-12

only on those with positional authority. When I think about significant developments in achieving any fundamental and civil rights across the globe, most have been ignited by grassroots campaigns by people with no positional authority. Think about it, when the world was at a standstill and finally acknowledged the inequities in policing after witnessing the murder of George Floyd, everyday people cried out for justice and change. We finally began to see the progress inside and outside the workplace in eradicating systemic racism. So, no matter what your role is in the workplace, you play a big part. So take notes.

It begins with *EMPATHY.*

Up to now, I have written a great deal about the various inequitable ways people view mental health versus physical health in the workplace. I won't continue to belabor the point, but the truth is hard to argue. It is a BIG issue. In the first part of this book, you took a walk in my shoes as a capable, confident, and educated person diagnosed with a mental health condition. I shared every raw detail of this moment so that you could understand the ins and outs of this disease. Empathy, the ability to share and understand the feelings of another, comes much easier when you have insights into the situation they are experiencing. I will be the first to admit that, before being diagnosed, I hadn't taken the time to understand mental health conditions, even when they affected my husband, son, sister, and other family members. So, it was difficult for me to share or understand what they were going through. What I exhibited was sympathy, which is starkly different from empathy. I pitied them. I felt sorry for them. But I didn't truly immerse myself in what they were experiencing.

After I experienced my mental health crisis and began to share my diagnosis with my family, friends, and colleagues, I noticed that much of their thinking went to, "How is this news going to affect me?" Them, and not me who was the one with the diagnosis. This response was hurtful, and I didn't feel supported. Notice how the fallout with my family was rooted in them being sympathetic but not empathetic. They would say, "I'm sorry this happened to you, but will you still be able to…" The same was true for my job at the mental health hospital. There was sympathy, I'll admit, but empathy was limited meaning the people I engaged in these conversations with showed pity, but not compassion and understanding. They also immediately assumed that I could not perform my job to the same level as before my diagnosis. The organization discouraged me from talking about my diagnosis in the workplace, and I felt isolated and excluded, something I had never felt before. Reflecting on my experience and the experiences of people who have shared similar experiences about the same reactions from their families and workplaces, here is how to cultivate empathy for mental health struggles at work. This is our first step in fostering equity.

Awareness and Candor

The more you know about mental health conditions, the more you can demonstrate empathy. We can empathize with physical health conditions and struggles because people are more willing to discuss them openly and are most often armed with more knowledge. Millions of social media platforms, websites, and blogs are dedicated to the journeys of people experiencing them. Whether it is battling obesity, cancer, or even commonly accepted mental health conditions such as Alzheimer's or dementia, we understand what people who have been diagnosed with these conditions are going through, and we empathize. We want the best outcome for their condition.

But leveling the playing field to achieve equity through awareness means that those of us experiencing struggles with our mental health have to take off our masks and discuss the challenges we face in the workplace. To do this, we must be intrinsically in tune with our minds and candid when something doesn't feel quite right. At least for us. Whether someone is struggling with their mental health or knows someone who is, talking about it can be one of the most difficult things to do, and we have already outlined why. However, to understand where the inequities exist in the workplace for people struggling with their mental health, having the ability to be transparent about mental health challenges is a must. Recall, one of the inequities I experienced upon returning from leave after my mental health crisis was that the person filling in for me continued to "help" me with my job responsibilities. In my many years in human resources, I have never seen this happen after someone returned from a leave of absence unless the person only returned intermittently. Sure, there may be a brief period of transition, but that usually only lasts a couple of days. Plus, this person was already employed in the same health system, so I could have easily contacted her with any questions. But this was not the case. Somewhere down the line, it was decided that I couldn't do the exceptional job I had always done before my stay in a mental health hospital.

Being able to return to work after a mental illness diagnosis and be seen as a competent professional meant the world to me. It would affirm, in my mind at least, that the perception of myself had not changed. In my case, candor from my new manager about his doubts regarding my capabilities could have saved both sides from poor miscommunication, humiliation, and self-doubt. Admittedly, I also could have approached the situation differently. I followed the standard process for requesting an accommodation to work remotely under the A.D.A. (Americans with Disabilities Act). Like many other organizations, this process involved my doctor completing a form giving his medical recommendation for the accommodation, submitting it to the Workforce Safety and Health Office, the Workforce Safety and Health Office discussing my accommodation with my manager, and, finally, I would be informed whether my accommodation had been approved. A direct conversation between my manager and myself was missing from the process. Looking back, it wouldn't have hurt for me to pick up the phone and reassure my manager that although I was requesting a minor accommodation of working remotely (which was still the norm for most of the office employees at that time), I was ready to jump back into my responsibilities full speed ahead. Because I didn't address my perceptions of being treated unfairly promptly after my return, I began to self-stigmatize myself. And

95

with each passing day, my ability to return to the competent, capable, and confident person I was before being diagnosed diminished rapidly. A simple phone call could have more than likely helped me to reclaim my mental health at work.

I am not proposing that people should always disclose their mental health status to their employers. In most countries, you do not have to, and your employer is not permitted to ask you (more on that later in this chapter). But I am proposing that if you have been diagnosed with a mental health condition or are struggling with your mental health and there is something that needs to be said or done outside of the standard scope of your organization's policies and procedures, take action! Speaking out may save you from going deeper into a mental health crisis and force your organization to change its current way of addressing things. As the adage goes, "you can't help those who won't help themselves."

When my non-profit, The Bowman Foundation, conducted our survey on the current state of mental health in the workplace, we were provided with many examples of people successfully engaging in conversations about their mental health with their employers.

For instance, one respondent said, "My direct leader at the time helped me get into therapy. I talked about my mental health diagnosis in an interview for a position I currently hold and got the job!"

Another wrote, "I was able to self-identify as someone with a disability. My immediate supervisor was incredibly supportive throughout this process and even though I identify as a person with a disability, I was recently promoted to a high-level role."

Again, "You don't get what you don't ask for." Candor is one of the most vital components to fostering equity in the workplace, especially for managers. If you are approached by someone struggling with their mental health, do not retreat from the subject just because you are uncomfortable with it. Lean into it and be candid about what you know or don't know. The worst thing you can do is invalidate someone's feelings, make assumptions, and act on what you do not know much about.

Common Institutional/Structural Barriers

One of the most significant ways to foster equity in the workplace to promote mental wellness is to evaluate and remove institutional structural barriers. I listed the most common structural barriers to equity at the beginning of this chapter. Now, I will provide you with guidance on how to remove these barriers. This section is critically important if you are a decision-maker or a human resources team member.

Prioritizing Mental-Wellbeing within Your Organization

While there has been more focus on mental health in workplaces recently, much work is still needed to bridge the gap between the efforts and expenditures focused on physical and mental well-being. One way to achieve this is by re-examining time and attendance policies. The policies tend to penalize people who take unscheduled time off. This results in people showing up to work when they should engage in self-care. I understand that it is burdensome to find last-minute coverage for unscheduled absences, but it is even more burdensome to work when you're not well, and in some professions, it can even be dangerous. Creating safe spaces for discussing mental health is also important. I will provide guidance on how to engage in inclusive conversations about mental health later in this section.

Access to Mental Health Providers

During my years as an H.R. executive, I didn't once ensure that my workforce had access to mental health providers. What do I mean by that? I should have asked our medical benefits providers about the ratio between mental health providers and the number of employees who signed up for medical benefits. I assumed my employees were cared for because we provided an Employee Assistance Program (E.A.P.) and medical benefits. That was not the case for my former organizations and probably not the case for yours either. But first, I would like to start with a discussion about E.A.P.s. Most organizations rely solely on E.A.P.s when someone needs mental health assistance outside their medical benefits offerings. I have several issues with this reliance, leading me to recoin the acronym Empty Ass Promises. Here's why. Many E.A.P. programs only give each employee a nominal number of visits to a mental health provider. You typically don't get to choose who that provider is. And, by the time you get the opportunity to share everything that is going on with you, guess what? Your time's up—no more visits. Then, you're left to find your own provider. This is where things become significantly challenging.

Finding a mental health provider can still be daunting even if you have medical insurance. According to the National Council of Mental WellBeing, getting an appointment can take up to six weeks. If you need a provider specializing in specific mental health conditions (like me), your wait can stretch into months! If you don't have medical insurance, you will likely have to pay hundreds of dollars out of pocket. At one point, my husband was paying a psychiatrist $295 for fifteen minutes of services (which meant that the provider was only interested in writing a prescription rather than providing psychological care for him). Telehealth companies have been popping up over the past two years, which have helped to shorten the wait time for mental health care, but when it comes to these companies, I would advise caution.

I recently contacted one of these companies when I was experiencing a mental health crisis, and my primary mental health provider was not available. The company required me to first sign up for a monthly subscription and only then was I given access to choose a therapist from a list of profiles. I found one who I thought would be able to give me useful advice and made an appointment for the next day. Yay! Before attending the appointment, I was asked to complete a questionnaire. One of the questions asked me about my religion, and I answered that I didn't have one. Once I got on the call with the therapist and briefly told her what I was experiencing, she asked if I prayed. I informed her that I was not a woman of faith. For the remainder of the call, she insisted that I pray to solve my mental health condition. She even told me that some patients had cured their bipolar disorder through prayer and prayer alone. I must have missed that article in the *Journal of Psychiatric Medicine*! I left the session feeling more in a mental health crisis than when I started the phone call. I didn't feel seen or heard. I felt downright ignored. Although the platform strives to, in their own words, "make professional counseling accessible, affordable, convenient – so anyone who struggles with life's challenges can get help, anytime, anywhere," the fine print at the bottom of the page contradicts their so-called aim by stating, "*We cannot assess whether the use of the Counselor, the Counselor Services, or the Platform is right and suitable for your needs. THE PLATFORM DOES NOT INCLUDE THE PROVISION OF MEDICAL CARE, MENTAL HEALTH SERVICES, OR OTHER PROFESSIONAL SERVICES BY US.*" Yikes! This is very dangerous and misleading and, of course, very disappointing. When I shared this experience on LinkedIn, I was astounded by the number of people who shared similar disappointing experiences on this particular platform.

So, what should organizations do to ensure access to mental health care?

 The person responsible for making decisions regarding medical benefits for the organization should reach out to your medical benefits provider to determine the ratio of mental health providers to your workforce. If there is a low ratio of providers to workers, shop for other benefits providers before your next open enrollment. In addition to inquiring about ratios, ask about the diversity of those providers. People in marginalized groups have unique experiences that impact their mental health, and someone familiar with those experiences will more likely be able to provide them with the more culturally competent care.

✓ Because there is a global shortage of mental health providers, employers may have to expand their offerings outside their medical benefits network. Organizations can contract with a telehealth provider, but I would advise conducting a due diligence process to ensure that there is no surprising fine print like my experience I previously described.

✓ Optimize your relationship with your E.A.P. provider as well. Many of us who engage with E.A.P.s on behalf of our organizations need an ongoing relationship with them. We sign a contract year after year, but seldom ask questions about utilization rates, wait times for an employee to be connected with a provider, whether they assist employees with finding a provider outside of the E.A.P. network after their allotted sessions have concluded, and what may be the common themes raised by the workforce? That last question is critical because many organizations still need a considerable opportunity to use this data further to promote the mental well-being of their workforce. Of course, E.A.P.s cannot share individual data, but they can tell you if employees are experiencing some of the following:

   o Financial difficulties: this could signal that you should review your compensation and pay equity data.
   o Work-life challenges: this is an opportunity to revisit your flex time model if you have one or implement one if you do not.
   o Work culture issues: this is a big one! Are there leaders or other factors derailing your employees' mental health? If so, you need to take action to improve the situation.

If you are someone reading this book waiting to receive mental health care, please know that you can visit your primary care provider while you wait. Primary care providers likely are not equipped to give you therapy or psychiatric services, but they can determine if any underlying physical conditions may impact your mental health. They are also authorized to prescribe psychiatric medication in most states in the U.S.

Evaluating Performance and Upward Mobility

I previously told you about being strongly advised by my boss that I should refrain from speaking about my mental health crisis at work (which happened to be at a psychiatric hospital). When I read through the comments from the Current State of Mental Health in the Workplace survey administered by my non-profit, I learned that countless people have had something related to their mental health brought up in a performance evaluation. For example, one respondent on the survey wrote:

"During my performance review, I was [told] that I miss too much work, even though I had a doctor's diagnosis and medical exemption, and that I couldn't be relied [upon] on because of my 'emotional state.' Never mind that my diagnosis did not impact my work and I was still being relied on and given big projects to shepherd to completion. I was viewed differently, and it was used to deny promotions and raises even though my workload had gone up and I was still considered a high performer."

Another wrote,

"It was easy to get time off for appointments, but at my performance review, my manager's comments included [the number of times I had not worked a full week]"

The Current State of Mental Health in the Workplace survey was open to participants who lived and worked in the United States. In case you are not aware, it is illegal to discriminate or retaliate against someone because they have taken a job-protected leave or have a real or *perceived* disability. We will go deeper into the legal aspects of disability protections across the globe in a future chapter. Still, the point here is the practice of citing excessive absences due to someone's disability or the fact they have taken job-protected leave as a reason to give them a low-performance rating or are not considered for a promotion is illegal and must stop. Job-protected leaves, sick banks, and other forms of paid and protected time off from work should be encouraged, not discouraged, if organizations genuinely care about the mental well-being of their workforce.

Let's shift your perspective for a minute. During the COVID-19 pandemic, many people in particular professions could not work remotely. As a response, some organizations went as far as to check the temperature and other symptoms of COVID of their workers every day to ensure that they were well enough to be at work. Even if a worker showed only one symptom, mild or not, they were asked to stay home until they could prove that they were COVID-19 negative. At one point, test results took days to come back. But guess what? Managers waited patiently for those results before hounding their employees to return to work. If someone did test positive for COVID-19, they received 14 days off with pay. Paid time off was also given when a family member tested positive. A separate COVID-19 leave bank was required by law (at least in New York). At the end of 2020 and 2021, I didn't hear from one person saying that there was a reference to them being out too much with COVID-19 mentioned in their review. Managers were grateful that people were not at the workplace physically spreading a deadly virus!

Organizational leaders knew the dangers of COVID-19. They knew how awful it felt to be diagnosed with the virus and how quickly it could spread to others. Therefore, COVID-19 was an acceptable reason to be out of work, and special considerations were made to accommodate those who or whose family members had contracted it. The same must be done for mental health conditions. Suppose someone needs time away from work to improve their mental health. In that case, they should not face retaliation through low-performance ratings, being blocked from upward mobility, or even termination. This practice harms those who have experienced these unfair responses and it sends a vital sign to others that they should not take time off to care for their mental health.

People with mental health conditions, just like those without, can be high performers, and they deserve upward mobility. In contrast to popular opinion, studies have revealed that people with mental health conditions are extraordinary employees with even more extraordinary skill sets. For instance, according to a Forbes article, "ADHD: The Entrepreneurs Super Power," organizations should leverage the symptoms of ADHD, such as the ability to multitask and perform in crisis mode[19]. Another article pointed out how bipolar disorder is related to demonstrating empathy, a great leadership trait, and how OCD can "harness [a person's] ability to do things to perfection," which can all be to an organization's advantage. Countless founders and CEOs have been diagnosed with these mental health conditions and have made some of the most remarkable contributions to society, including big names such as Steve Jobs and Howard Hughes.

The point is, rather than immediately diving into punitive action against someone with a known mental health condition, it would be wiser to explore how their condition may be contributing to the success of the team or company. My undiagnosed bipolar disorder contributed significantly to my ability to be a successful businesswoman. I will be honest and admit that there were times when being undiagnosed and untreated did adversely affect a job or two. But now that I am diagnosed, I lean into the positive ways my brain works and manage the negative ways it plays out. I am ready for any challenge ahead of me, and so are you or the people in your organization who have also been diagnosed with mental health conditions.

---

[19] Dr. Dale Archer, ADHS: The Entrepreneur's Superpower, Forbes Magazine, May 14, 2014, https://www.forbes.com/sites/dalearcher/2014/05/14/adhd-the-entrepreneurs-superpower/?sh=9b7a08259e97

Pay Inequity

In the UK, "people who have been diagnosed with mental health problems such as depression and panic attacks earn up to 42% less than their peers."[20] In the U.S., "people with serious mental illness make an estimated $16,000 less per year than those without a serious mental illness."[21] However, more research is needed to determine if the pay disparity is due to discrimination or a lack of resources for those with mental health conditions. It is quite clear why this is the case. Most pay raises are based on your performance evaluation. If you are receiving low-performance ratings, you are unlikely to get a significant salary increase or promotion.

Additionally, many people come out of the workforce after suffering from a mental health crisis and are afraid to return because they know they will likely not be supported. Remember the stories I shared in Chapter One, "Real People, Real Stories"? Each person in those stories separated from their organization due to a mental health crisis; most never returned or were delayed. When you are out of work, you lose years of experience. Experience is taken into consideration when calculating your future salary. Therefore, similar to what has contributed to the wage gap for females, some of the same factors are true for those with mental health conditions. Imagine the pay inequities for someone like me who has intersecting identities of being Black, a

---

[20] Denis Campbell, UK's 'hidden disgrace': mental health problems can lead to 42% pay gap, The Guardian, August 6, 2016, https://www.theguardian.com/society/2016/aug/06/mental-health-pay-gap-depression-panic-attacks

[21] Denise Guerra and Samantha Masunaga, Bosses say they care about mental health—can workers trust them?, LA Times Business section, February 23, 2023, https://www.latimes.com/business/story/2023-02-23/mental-health-and-the-workplace

woman, and someone with a mental illness. It creates a specific set of challenges for me that can tend to put me in a battle with myself and my work environment as I strive for my personal excellence and mental wellbeing.

Pay inequities for people with mental health conditions often reflect broader systemic issues related to discrimination, lack of access to resources, and other social and economic factors. These systemic issues can perpetuate pay inequities and make it difficult for individuals with mental health conditions to access the same opportunities as those without mental health conditions.

As previously stated, one way we can end the pay gap for those with mental health conditions is to disassociate mental health conditions from performance ratings (unless the condition negatively impacts the person's performance). Another is to never inquire about a candidate's previous salary. This practice has been outlawed in a few states but should become the norm for every organization. Pay people for their worth and their job, not based on what they have been paid in the past. There are no apples to apples in any scenario. Lastly, some people with mental health conditions need special accommodations to perform. Instead of automatically dismissing someone due to their performance that may be impacted by a mental health condition, explore ways to develop, grow, and prepare them for the next level of their careers.

 Evaluate Your Policies and Processes

There are inherent inequities built into an organization's policies and processes, meaning how they operate. I gave one example when explaining how my former organization's accommodation process left out a critical component: a direct conversation between my manager and me. The result was that I was treated differently than other people when they returned from medical leave. However, other examples exist of how our current policies and processes can result in inequities for people with mental health conditions. For example, as with many policies, more than "one-to-many" is needed. What do I mean by "one-to-many"? I mean one policy that applies to an entire workforce. My lawyer friends are cringing right now because they will argue that this one-to-many concept will keep organizations out of legal trouble. One-to-many means that everyone is being treated equally. That there is consistency in the organization. Well, being consistent does not always equate to being fair. To be consistent is to equality. Fairness is equity. Equity is the opposite of equality. Again, equality assumes that everyone is playing on a level playing field, and we know that with humans with diverse backgrounds, that is not the case. To cultivate equitable work environments, organizations must become less stringent with dictating policies or allowing policies to dictate their culture rather than compassion and empathy. Some additional samples of processes and policies that should be re-examined include:

Flextime policies

While many organizations have attempted to address the mental health of their workforce by implementing flextime policies, most of these policies still need to catch up to their intent. For example, an organizational policy may say that employees should work at their worksite three days a week and remotely twice a week. While that sounds great and flexible, these policies are capricious and arbitrary. Why three days remote? What three days? What research did you conduct to determine that three days was the magic number? When some of my clients began calling their employees back to the office for a finite number of days, I asked them these questions. No client was able to give a clear answer. The best response was, "three days just felt right." I get it. There is an argument that there are advantages of in-person collaborations, building interpersonal relationships, and becoming more connected to the company culture when you are on-site. But how can that happen in a finite number of days?

Instead of arbitrarily implementing flextime policies with finiteness that applies to everyone, try this instead:

- Allow individual flexibility, meaning allowing employees to work from the office when they want to and when it makes sense.

- If you have specific days when employees are in the office, ensure that there is an opportunity to accomplish what you think having them back in the office can do. Will there be a team meeting that is open for collaboration? Will there be in-person professional development? Will a social event be taking place that connects people or the company culture?

- Allow managers to determine what makes sense for their teams. If a manager is okay with their teams working 100% remotely, let them make that call. But I advise senior management and H.R. to have discussions with each manager, asking them to justify their decisions. That way, if one department is allowed more flexibility than others, you know why and can be transparent about those decisions.

- Define clear performance expectations. If employees meet defined performance goals, you know your workplace flexibility models are working. Without clear expectations, you are just making arbitrary decisions that can result in losing some of your best talents.

In short, many organizations are demanding that their workforce returns to the office because they lack trust in their employees, despite research indicating that when employees are provided this type of flexibility, they are more productive, their performance improves, and they are happier, more committed, and loyal[22].

[22] Laurel Farer, 5 Proven Benefits of Remote Work for Companies, Forbes Magazine, February 12, 2020, https://www.forbes.com/sites/laurelfarrer/2020/02/12/top-5-benefits-of-remote-work-for-companies/?sh=35b1135216c8

Organizations have even seen higher profitability. Lack of trust in employees is one of the critical components of disengagement, demotivation, and unhappiness at work. You hired your team to do a job. Trust them to do it unless they give you a reason not to.

 ## Workplace Accommodations

Workplace accommodations are a legal right for people diagnosed with a mental illness and are considered disabled or perceived disabled in many countries. However, these accommodations are often granted inequitably. The main reason for this inequity is that it is sometimes easier to understand that an accommodation is needed when the disability is visible rather than invisible, as would be the case for accommodations related to mental health. For instance, if someone needs an alternative keyboard, that's easy; you call I.T. and get it. However, when a workplace disability accommodation requires more thought, creativity, and flexibility, inequities happen. Someone shared with me that they requested a workplace accommodation to be seated where there is more sunlight to help treat their seasonal depression. The only available place where their request could be accommodated was in a corridor where the senior executives sat. Her request was denied because her company couldn't have this "rank-n-file," "low-level employee" sitting with executives. You had to have a specific "title" to sit in an office with windows with executives. That sounds silly, right? But it happens all the time. The Americans with Disabilities Act, along with most, if not all, other workplace disability laws across the globe, could care less what your title is. Still, unfortunately, many organizations take your title or place on the organizational hierarchy when considering what accommodations they will grant someone.

Summary of Guidance

Institutional/Structural Barrier	Guidance on Dismantling the Inequity
Prioritizing Mental-Wellbeing	Prioritizing mental well-being requires organizations to create a supportive work culture, provide mental health benefits, promote work-life harmony, provide training and education, and create a safe and respectful work environment.
Access to Mental Health Providers	Adequate, immediate access to mental health care is essential for promoting the overall well-being of employees, reducing absenteeism and presenteeism, increasing employee engagement and retention, and reducing stigma around mental health.
Evaluating Performance and Upward Mobility	In most cases, mental health conditions are irrelevant to an employee's ability to perform their job duties. Therefore, it is not appropriate for employers to consider mental health when evaluating performance or upward mobility.

Pay Inequities	Various factors, including discrimination, underemployment, lack of accommodations, limited access to healthcare, and systemic issues, can cause pay inequities for people with mental health conditions.
Policies and Processes	It is essential for employers to not have stringent policies and processes that are assumed to be accommodating to all employees at all times. Policies and processes should be equitable and inclusive and should involve providing a flexible working environment and workplace accommodations.
Flexibility and Accommodations	Flexible work arrangements and creative accommodations can help reduce stress by allowing employees to better manage their work-life harmony.

CHAPTER 9

AWARENESS

I went decades without knowing I was living with a mental health condition. As I wrote in Part I of this book, when I went through my first bipolar hyper manic episode, I thought I was just being a rebellious twenty-something-year-old. When it happened again, I thought I was reacting to being a new wife and mother to a baby. The third time I thought I was going through a midlife crisis. When I was in hypomania, which I now know is my normal state of being, I thought I just had the energy of the Energizer Bunny Rabbit and the confidence of Beyoncè. I knew I could extend my capacity to do things more than the average person, but it just never occurred to me that I may have a medical condition. Now that I know I have a mental health condition, my life has forever changed. And believe it or not, it's changed for the better. I am keenly aware of how my mind operates and how my physical health and environment impact my mental health. Most importantly, the people close to me are aware of my triggers and behaviors to help me protect my mental health.

The first step to finding happiness at work is to acknowledge that you may be struggling with your mental health. Next, you must understand that part of cultivating cultures of mental wellness in the workplace means that you can identify if someone you're working with may be struggling with their mental health as well and be able to provide them the support that they need. Finally, there needs to be a heightened awareness of the environmental factors that may impact your mental health. So, with that, we will discuss awareness from three perspectives:

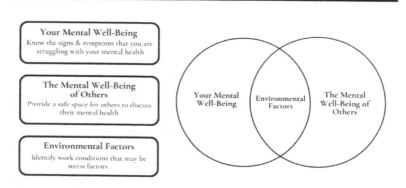

- Your Mental Well-Being
- The Mental Well-Being of Others
- Environmental Factors

Your Mental Well-Being

One question I often receive is, "Natasha, how do I know if someone is struggling with their mental health, is having a bad day, or just doesn't want to be bothered?" I have bad days occasionally, but that doesn't mean I am slipping into a bipolar disorder depressive state. I also have days where I am extraordinarily energetic and happy, but that doesn't mean I'm going into a bipolar manic state. As humans, we all experience tremendous emotions throughout our day. We've all had days that we've woken up extremely positive and happy about the day ahead, and then something or someone manages to change our mood at some point. At that point, we just want to be left alone to drink our coffee, read through our emails, and maybe lose ourselves on TikTok for a minute or two. After getting our thoughts together, we may return to our positive state of mind, or we may just mark that day as a bad one and count down the hours until we can go home, Netflix, and chill. In that scenario, you're probably not experiencing a mental health crisis. You're just experiencing life. Shit happens. While this book is not intended to give medical advice, you should be aware of signs that you may be struggling with your mental health rather than just having a bad day.

According to the Mayo Clinic[23], examples of signs and symptoms that you may be dealing with a mental health condition include:

- feeling sad or down
- confused thinking or reduced ability to concentrate
- excessive fears or worries, or extreme feelings of guilt
- extreme mood changes of highs and lows
- withdrawal from friends and activities
- significant tiredness, low energy, or problems sleeping
- detachment from reality (delusions), paranoia, or hallucinations
- inability to cope with daily problems or stress
- trouble understanding and relating to situations and people
- problems with alcohol or drug use
- major changes in eating habits
- sex drive changes
- excessive anger, hostility, or violence
- suicidal thinking

---

[23] Mental Illness, Mayo Clinic, https://www.mayoclinic.org/diseases-conditions/mental-illness/symptoms-causes/syc-20374968, accessed on March 20, 2023.

Additionally, mental health conditions can present as physical symptoms as well, such as "stomach pain, back pain, headaches, or other unexplained aches and pains."[24] Even with that information, you're probably still wondering if you're experiencing a mental health crisis or just having a couple of bad days. Let me explain a little further. While both can be distressing and impact our well-being, a mental health crisis is a situation beyond your ability to cope with and may require immediate intervention to ensure your safety. A bad day, on the other hand, is a normal part of life that we all experience from time to time. It can be triggered by various stressors, such as work or relationship problems, resulting in sadness, frustration, or irritability.

In contrast, a mental health crisis typically involves intense and overwhelming feelings that can result in a loss of control or an inability to cope. Examples of mental health crises include suicidal thoughts, panic attacks, psychosis, or extreme mood swings. It is important to note that a mental health crisis can develop gradually over time. Recognizing warning signs and seeking early intervention is essential to prevent the crisis from escalating.

Some ways that you can use to potentially avoid both bad days and a mental health crisis is to engage in actively taking care of your mental hygiene. Mental hygiene is defined as the science of maintaining mental health and preventing disorders to help people function at their full mental potential. It includes all measures taken to promote and preserve mental health: rehabilitation of the mentally disturbed, prevention of mental illness, and aid in coping in a stressful world. If you're like most people, you have primary health providers for other parts of your anatomy. You are comfortable with them because you've established a relationship with them, they know and have documented your medical history, and they are likely just a phone call away in case of a medical emergency. The same can be true for proactively establishing a relationship with a mental health provider *before* a mental health crisis. Once I finally established a relationship with one, I was

---

[24] Ibid.

shocked to learn about how all of my unaddressed trauma had been impacting not just my mental health but how I dealt with certain aspects of my life in an unhealthy way. Since then, I've always wondered how better I would have dealt with specific periods and circumstances of my life if I had been more proactive with addressing my mental health as I had my physical health. As you explore some ways to maintain your mental hygiene, reflect on these questions:

? What are some of the daily things you do to maintain your physical health and appearance? Do you brush your teeth and comb your hair?
? Do you typically wait until you get a toothache before you see a dentist, or do you visit a dentist annually for a preventive check-up?
? Do you go to your primary care physician for an annual physical to check your blood work, blood pressure, weight management, etc.?
? Do you go for an annual GYN exam?
? Do you go for a prostate exam?
? How often do you go to the gym?
? How often do you get a haircut, get your nails done, have your feet scrubbed, and get a facial?

I know that last one seems petty but think about it. We invest a lot of time and energy into our physical health and appearance. We are super proactive about these things because we are well aware of what can happen if we aren't (I do not want to be caught slipping with crusty feet, especially in the summertime!). If you're reading this book, being proactive may be too late. You may already be experiencing the symptoms that I listed at the beginning of this section. When do you need to seek medical attention? No time is better than the present. No one knows you better than you, especially about your emotions, feelings, and behaviors. Remember, those changes to your behavior may not even be what we typically think of when we think of struggling with our mental health. For example, when I am in a bipolar hypomanic episode, I am extremely happy, confident, productive, and creative. That sounds like a perfect state of being, right? But the key word here is *extremely*. Happily, working until 3 AM is not healthy. So, if you're not feeling like yourself in any way, shape, or form, it's long past the time to check on your mental health.

Other ways to practice healthy mental hygiene include:

- Prioritize self-care: Engage in self-care activities that you enjoy, such as exercise, meditation, yoga, or spending time with friends and family. Prioritizing self-care can help you manage stress and maintain a positive outlook.

- Practice mindfulness: Mindfulness involves paying attention to the present moment, without judgment. Practicing mindfulness can help you manage stress and improve your overall well-being. Consider taking a mindfulness meditation class or using a mindfulness app.

- Practice good sleep hygiene: Getting enough sleep is important for mental health. Practice good sleep hygiene by creating a regular sleep routine, avoiding screens before bedtime, and keeping your sleeping environment comfortable and dark.

- Seek support: Reach out to friends, family, or mental health professionals for support when needed. It is important to ask for help when you need it and not feel ashamed to do so.

- Limit stressors: Identify stressors in your life and take steps to limit them. For example, if your job is a major source of stress, consider talking to your supervisor about ways to reduce your workload or seeking out a new job. (We'll talk more about this later).

- Engage in positive self-talk: Positive self-talk involves focusing on your strengths and accomplishments rather than dwelling on negative thoughts or self-criticism.

Encouraging and positive self-talk can help improve self-esteem and confidence.

The Mental Well-Being of Others

Picture this. Your coworker Nancy is one of the most positive, outgoing, and optimistic colleagues you've ever worked with. You've worked alongside her for almost five years. You're not the closest of colleagues, but you know her well enough to know that for the past few weeks, she doesn't seem to be herself. Instead of coming in and enjoying a cup of coffee and chatting with the team, she goes straight to her workstation and starts working. There's no more banter and when she does talk, she complains about work. She has never done this in the past. You're worried about her, but don't quite know how to approach her. Maybe you're Nancy's boss and you've noticed the same thing, plus you've noticed a decline in her job performance. Whether you're someone's colleague or manager, you're not alone in being fearful of approaching someone who may be struggling with their mental health. Addressing someone else's mental health can be just as scary as addressing your own mental health. Will they be offended? Will sharing your concern make matters worse? You'll probably take the route that most of us have taken of just minding your business and sending them thoughts and prayers. Or, if you're a manager, you may just address their performance without addressing that you've observed a difference in their non-work-related behavior. But I encourage you to follow your instincts and take the chance and express your concern.

When I was hospitalized after my suicide attempt, my mother came to town to help my husband and support him with my young daughter, but she was also able to come and visit me. Because I was hospitalized during the height of the COVID pandemic, I was only allowed one visitor a day so she and my husband would rotate their days. Either way, it was exciting to have a familiar face there. However, the first day my mom arrived, I was very nervous and anxious. For the past almost twenty years, I had wanted her to perceive me as perfect. I was the daughter who went from being a single mom to becoming a lawyer, professor, business owner, and author. I was the daughter that took her mother on vacations and Broadway plays when she was in town. Now, here I was sitting in a mental health hospital, which I still needed to explain to her. There were a lot of events that led to the suicide attempt that I was (and still am not) proud of. However, now was the time that I would have her full attention to talk about my mental health. Not just how the pandemic had affected it, but how some of the things that I had experienced in my childhood had triggered a trauma response that I hadn't been aware of until getting treatment. It would be an uncomfortable conversation, but now was a better time than ever to have it. While my mother and I spent a lot of time together in the past, I rarely shared anything about my personal life with her. During my mental health crisis, I figured out why.

After each experience that I shared with my mother, she responded that she had experienced something similar and would then share her story. These were supposed to be the moments when I could finally share how growing up with an alcoholic father and being inappropriately touched by my father's best friend, who also was a police officer, whom I had known since I was born, had created unresolved childhood trauma for me. But the moments turned into just "girlfriends" swapping stories. When she left, I felt unseen, unheard, and unsupported. When I was discharged and she left to go back home about a week later, we never spoke of my suicide attempt or anything I shared with her in the hospital again. Eventually, we would become completely estranged.

I share that story with you so that you could understand the perspective of someone who was struggling with their mental health and had the courage to share their struggles with someone to gain their support. Not everyone who is struggling with their mental health will always be in that place of mind, but many of us are. At that moment, I needed and expected my mother to do several things to support me on my journey

- First, I needed her to completely lean into what I was saying and what I was feeling until I was ready for a response. During the conversation, I felt as if I couldn't get a thought out without being interrupted by her sharing her thoughts and experiences.
- I needed my feelings to be validated. Of course, she knew my father was an alcoholic and I witnessed him do some things that a child under ten shouldn't have to see. But those things were never spoken of at home. Instead, we were just told to "keep our business out of the streets." This was a perfect opportunity for her to acknowledge that what I witnessed and experienced was unacceptable for a little girl.
- I also expected her to be surprised that I didn't reach out to her in the days leading to my suicide attempt. She's always acted as if we were "best friends." If that was the case, however, then "why hadn't I reached out to her?" Why was I willing to take my life before getting support from her? There was absolutely no curiosity about why I didn't think she would have been able to give me the support I needed.
- After I was home and "appeared" to be back to normal, she never checked back in on me regarding my mental health. Our conversations went back to business as usual until the conservatorship fiasco.

I hope you learned some key dos and don'ts about speaking with someone about their mental health from my experience, but in case you missed them, here are some key considerations. My case was slightly different from Nancy's in that I was definitely in a mental health crisis. In Nancy's case, you're not sure what's going on with her and your relationship is different as well. So, what I'll share will cover both scenarios as a general rule of thumb:

 Don't hesitate to approach someone who appears to be struggling with their mental health.

I don't know about you, but I'd rather someone be upset with me about asking than for someone to feel unsupported and in a potentially life-threatening crisis moment. Also, if you approach the person in a sensitive and compassionate way, there shouldn't be an issue, even if they don't want to share their struggles. Saying phrases such as:

"You don't seem to be your normal, happy, optimistic self lately. Is there something I can help you with? I know it's been bananas around here lately."

"Hey, I miss having coffee with you in the mornings! Is there something going on? You want to talk?"

" I know we're not that close, but I must admit that I've always appreciated the positive energy you bring to the office. However, I've been missing that lately. I'd love to bring some positive energy to you the way you have to me. Is there something I can help you with or do you want to have lunch today?"

Most people would not be offended by those statements. Even if they don't want to go into specifics about their situation, they will appreciate you showing concern and may just say, "I'm going through some personal challenges right now, but I'll be okay." Even though they don't want to share the specifics, you still may have had a significant impact on how they move forward. For example, they may not have even realized that their demeanor had shifted, or maybe they had been ignoring their current emotions and needed someone to nudge them to acknowledge that they are not themselves. Who knows? Sometimes, it takes someone else to point out that something's changed in you for you to see it. In the worst-case scenario, you've shown someone that you care about them. How powerful is that?

 If someone shares with you that they are struggling with their mental health

If Nancy or anyone else shares with you that they are struggling with their mental health, the following dos and don'ts are crucial for them to feel supported at that moment. Admitting that you are struggling with your mental health is one of the most vulnerable things that a person can do.

Engaging in Conversations with a Peer Struggling with Their Mental Health

Do	Don't
Listen to Learn	Immediately share your struggles or the experiences of someone you know. Everyone's experience is different, so listen to learn about that person's specific experience.
Ask meaningful questions	After you've given the person an opportunity to share what they are going through, don't be afraid to ask questions about things you don't understand. That shows the person that you are genuinely engaged in the conversation and concerned about their well-being.
Don't Pathologize	We are all "Google Doctors," meaning we think we know a lot about medical conditions based on what we've read on the internet. Once someone shares their struggles, don't try to diagnose them.
Validate their feelings	Don't argue with someone about how they are feeling. Their feelings are their feelings, whether you feel they are valid or not.

Ask how you can support them	Don't make assumptions about what kind of support that the person needs from you. Ask them specifically how you can support them. Don't overstep boundaries in the process.
Make suggestions for support and resources	If you have access or knowledge about additional support and resources, offer it on them.

If you are managing someone who you believe is struggling with their mental health, having a conversation with them about it can be even more complex. As I've stated earlier, as an HR professional, my colleagues and I advised managers not to engage in conversations with employees about their mental health. Why? Because we didn't trust managers to say or do the right things and saying the wrong thing can put the organization in legal jeopardy. Recently, I've changed my perspective on this. Instead, I encourage managers to have a direct, transparent relationship with their employees about all the aspects of the employee's life cycle. In fact, I've spent hundreds, maybe thousands, of hours coaching managers on how to have crucial and necessary conversations with their teams regarding their performance, career mobility, interpersonal relationships, etc. When they ask me if I am going to be present for these conversations, I've always said, "No, this is not my job. Your job as a manager is to manage your employee. Do it. I'm here for advice and guidance." Every single one of these conversations comes with a legal risk. For instance, someone could claim that their performance rating was based on race or that they didn't get a promotion because of their age. We must stop discouraging managers from engaging in difficult conversations to avoid legal liability, especially when it comes to mental health. In my opinion, there is a bigger liability if we don't engage in these conversations and that risk is losing top performers that simply need some additional support for usually a limited amount of time.

Managers must acknowledge when someone isn't performing or behaving in a way that they normally would. The guidance that I gave earlier doesn't change. As a manager, if I notice that someone's performance is declining, I recognize that poses a different challenge. My number one piece of advice is to never approach a conversation about job performance in a punitive manner. That goes for someone who is or isn't struggling with their mental health. If someone started in their role as a high performer, and you see their performance decline, there is usually another reason for it other than they just don't care about the job anymore. They usually have too much on their plate, competing priorities, dealing with a personal issue, or the work environment (I'll share more on that later), or has something else distracting them from performing at their normal level. In this situation, always approach someone about their declining performance with concern rather than hostility. Believe me, you're going to have a better outcome that way.

If you've learned that their declining performance is due to them struggling with their mental health, DO NOT immediately dismiss them to HR or EAP as the *ONLY* solution. Think back to my experience of the miss to have a direct conversation with my manager about what I needed (and didn't need) from them in terms of support, which resulted in an undesirable outcome. Do not "outsource" the mental health of your team. HR is there to advise about their legal rights. We are not mental health counselors, believe it or not. EAP also has a limited scope of what they can provide as well. Your organization may even have a company that assists with disability accommodations. While you can still follow your organization's processes, that doesn't discount going through the chart above about *how to engage in conversations with someone struggling with their mental health* without breaking any laws or policies. Believe me!

I realize that most managers are never given any guidance on the laws that govern mental disabilities in the workplace. You'd be surprised to know that the U.S. was one of the first, if not the first country, to pass federal legislation in 1990 for people working with disabilities. Since 2000, 181 countries have passed disability civil rights laws inspired by the ADA. While many of these laws address physical disabilities, I will break down the key highlights of the disability laws addressing mental disabilities across the globe starting with the U.S., and then show how other countries compare. Note, these laws apply to the private sector only in their respective countries.

United States - Americans with Disabilities Act of 1990, as amended (ADA)

- The ADA defines disability as a physical or mental impairment that substantially limits one or more major life activities.
- The ADA also prohibits discrimination against individuals who have a record (history) of a psychiatric disability or are regarded as having a psychiatric disability. Applicants and employees with psychiatric disabilities have two main rights under the ADA. First, they have the right to privacy, except for when asking for an accommodation. Second, they have the right to a job accommodation unless this causes undue hardship for the employer.

Australia- Disability Discrimination Act (DDA)
Key Differences from the ADA

- Very similar to the protections under the ADA, but also past and potential future disabilities are included in these protections.

The Commonwealth - Disability Discrimination Act (DDA)
Key Differences from the ADA

- Very similar to the protections under the ADA.
- It covers mental illness: whether temporary or permanent past, present or future actual or imputed.
- The law defines discrimination to include both direct and indirect discrimination. An example of indirect discrimination is:
  - An employer requires that employees must work an 8-hour shift but does not allow a worker with

124

mental illness to take additional breaks where required to be able to complete their shift.

Canada- Employment Equity Act (EEA)
Key Differences from the ADA

- Very similar to the protections under the ADA.
- People associated with persons with disabilities are also protected from discrimination and harassment. This could include family, friends, or someone advocating on a person's behalf.

Hong Kong - Disability Discrimination Ordinance
Key Differences from the ADA

- Less extensive protections than the ADA
- So long as an employee can perform the inherent requirements of a job, the employer is prohibited from terminating the employment on the ground of the disability.
- Hong Kong is starting to expect employers to take "reasonable care" as it relates to the mental health of its workforce. For example:

> An employee was awarded damages after suffering a work-related stress breakdown. In holding the school liable for the breach of the duty of care, the House of Lords noted that "the senior management team should have made inquiries about his problems and seen what they could do to ease them" given that the reason for the employee's absence as certified by the doctor was stress and depression[25]. The House of Lords did not accept

---

[25] Hong Kong – Mental Wellness And The Workplace – What Can And Should Employers Be Doing?, Press Release from Conventus Law, December 8, 2021, https://conventuslaw.com/report/hong-kong-mental-wellness-and-the-workplace-what/.

that termination or resignation were the only options. Rather, the senior management could have taken steps to make sympathetic enquires and reduction of the employee's workload.

United Kingdom (excluding Northern Ireland) - The Equality Act 2010
Key Differences from the ADA

- There are some substantial differences between the ADA and The Equality Act
- It defines disability as having a physical or mental impairment that has a "substantial" and "long-term" negative effect on the ability to engage in daily activities.
- "Long-term" means 12 months or more.
- Addiction to non–prescribed drugs or alcohol is not included in the definition of disability (it is under the ADA).

Environmental Factors

After speaking with someone about their mental health, you may learn during that conversation, that there is something about their work environment (including you) that is either causing them to struggle with their mental health or is exasperating their existing condition. Although I've just shared with you the various legal protections for employees with mental health conditions, organizations shouldn't rely on laws to cultivate cultures of mental wellness. The World Health Organization (WHO) recently published Mental Health at Work guidelines.[26] They have acknowledged that sustaining mental wellness in the workplace has become a global issue and organizations have had little to no

---

[26] Mental Health at Work, World Health Organization, September 22, 2022, https://www.who.int/news-room/fact-sheets/detail/mental-health-at-work#:~:text=Decent%20work%20is%20good%20for,a%20mental%20disorder%20in%202019, accessed on March 21, 2023.

guidance on how to create and sustain healthy and safe working conditions. According to WHO, to prevent work-related mental health conditions, you must manage psychosocial risks. Now, you're probably wondering what psychosocial risks are. A couple of examples that may ring a bell for you are inflexible work environments, harassment and discrimination, and poor management. Remember the story of Biljana that I shared in the "Real People, Real Stories" section of this book? If you don't, here's a quick reminder. Biljana was a high performer, but a due to a change in leadership she experienced a toxic work environment that included having her co-workers monitor and report on her performance, productivity, and anything else she did during the day, including counting how many times she went to the restroom! It was impossible for her to maintain sound mental health in such an environment. I've shared many stories of those who have been negatively impacted by their work environment. You get the point, so I won't share any more here. But what I will share are some common environmental psychosocial risks that are present in most workplaces and what employers can do to mitigate them.

Psychosocial Risk	Prevention
Lack of Empathy from Managers	Management training on mental health conditions, specifically to bridge the gap between the perspectives between physical and mental health
Micromanagement/ Lack of Trust	People are hired to do a job, let them do it. If they need more development to their jobs, give them development, not uncomfortable oversight.
Discrimination	People in marginalized groups are more likely to experience toxic

	work environments. Inclusion efforts should be prioritized.
Lack of Accountability	There should be no "untouchables" within your organization. Untouchables are those that engage in discriminatory behaviors, bullying, harassment, and incivility and the organization has full knowledge of their conduct, but fails to address them.
The Socio-Political Environment	There is a strong correlation between what happens in the socio/political environment and people's experiences at work. Addressing traumatic events in the external environment shows that you are not tone deaf and care about your employee's overall well-being, not just what's happening at work.
Interpersonal Relationships	Interpersonal relationships play a huge role in the workplace environment. One of the biggest threats to positive interpersonal relationships is the lack of diversity and cultural competency. Organizations that lack diversity and cultural competency tend to create exclusive experiences for the non-majority through insensitive words, actions, and behaviors. Recruiting a diverse workforce and conducting training on cultural competency is key to developing strong interpersonal relationships.

As you can see, the workplace environmental factors that are negatively impacting the mental health of workers across the globe are hiding in plain sight. What you have read in the chart shouldn't be breaking news to you. More likely than not, you have either experienced one or more of these risks, or one or more of these have been reported to you. However, despite the awareness of how much these factors create toxic and hostile work environments across demographics, organizations have allowed them to perpetuate, and workers have tolerated or accepted them as the norm. Now is the time to shift this perspective and not allow our work cultures to risk our overall health. I say overall health because our mental health impacts our physical health and vice versa. If you are a decision-maker reading this book, then you have the privilege to apply the intervention methods that have been recommended. If you're an individual contributor, then you have the privilege to demand better. Think you can't or don't know how? Think again. I'll be sharing those tips with you later on in the book.

What we can conclude from the Awareness part of the F.A.M.E. framework is that now is the time for employers to revisit their employee wellbeing policies, think beyond the traditional health benefits and perks, take into account the international instruments for employee wellbeing, and redefine the employee well-being policies that put equal emphasis on employees' mental health like physical health.

Employee well-being is no more limited to physical health, lifestyle, and earnings; it is more about the work culture, job satisfaction, and connection with the leadership.

CHAPTER 10

MANAGING BURNOUT

Imagine you light a match and it burns until the flame goes out. What are you able to do with that match now? Absolutely nothing. But if you blow out the match before it burns out, you may be able to reuse it and even use it to light other matches or ignite other things. In the workplace, people are like matches. They are on fire. Sometimes that fire is used for good, or sometimes that fire is the beginning of the end. Fires can ignite innovation, passion, and excitement in workplaces, or our fires can be used as weapons of mass destruction.

In many cases, we experience both. We begin our jobs and careers with a fire meant to ignite something special, but eventually, we feel like we are the ones who have been set on fire, waiting for our demise. When the latter is the case, we experience burnout.

I've heard many people throw out the phrase they are burned out, but I am not sure they understand what it means to be burned out. According to WHO, "Burnout is a syndrome conceptualized as resulting from chronic workplace stress that has not been successfully managed."[27] Three dimensions characterize it:

- feelings of energy depletion or exhaustion
- increased mental distance from one's job, feelings of negativism or cynicism related to one's job
- reduced professional efficacy

That last bullet point has been recoined as engaging in "quiet quitting," which sounds sexier than reduced professional efficacy. Either way, once someone is burned out, they become useless to themselves or their organization. There are four phases of fire development and depletion: ignition, growth, fully developed, and decay. The phases of burnout are similar to the phases that a person experiences from when they first enter the workplace to eventually feeling burned out.

Phase 1 - Ignition: You've started a new job or project. You can't wait to prove to your organization and peers your worth. You "hit the ground running" and pour everything you have into your new role and assignment. You even find yourself enthusiastically bringing this work home to meet or beat deadlines. Perfection is what you are aiming towards. Perfection leads to self-efficacy, praise from your manager, peer acknowledgment, and upward mobility. You are fueled by fulfillment, motivation, passion and promise. With these attributes, you believe you have everything you need, you are fully ignited, and your fire begins.

Phase 2 - Growth: You begin to notice that the enthusiasm you share about your new role or project is now shared by others. You

---

[27] Burn-out an "occupational phenomenon": International Classification of Diseases, World Health Organization, May 28, 2019, https://www.who.int/news/item/28-05-2019-burn-out-an-occupational-phenomenon-international-classification-of-diseases, accessed March 21, 2023.

are beginning to be bombarded by other projects and responsibilities that take up a lot of time, but you're determined to blow whatever you are doing out of the water. Regardless of the additional responsibilities and tasks, your fire is growing, and it is still burning ferociously.

Phase 3 - Fully Developed: You have a lot on your plate. Your cup runneth over. You are still meeting every deadline for every project or task. You are skipping lunch and taking work home. You are determined to manage it all. You have set out to prove something and are determined to do it. Your fire is fully developed as you release the highest heat rate you can produce.

Phase 4 - Decay Stage: During the decay stage, the heat and the intensity for what you are working on are finally reduced. All of the available fuel that you once had has been consumed. You have received no support, resources, or acknowledgment from your manager that you're overwhelmed, yet the expectation that you complete every task, project, and assignment is still expected. Your fuel, which had initially come in the form of motivation, acknowledgment, and support from your manager, peer support, and self-efficacy, is gone. You are officially burned out.

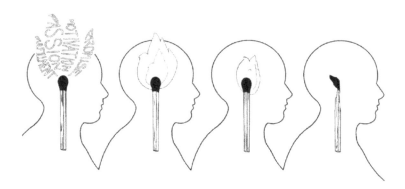

Being burned out is more severe than once thought. In 2019, WHO declared burnout as a "syndrome that results from 'chronic workplace stress that has not been successfully managed'" and even classified it as an occupational phenomenon specifically related to the workplace[28]. Christine Sinsky, MD, Vice President of Professional Satisfaction at the American Medical Association (AMA), stated, "Burnout is primarily related to the environment, such as when there is a mismatch between the workload and the resources needed to do the work in a meaningful way." In many situations, we must keep going in our jobs until we reach this burnout phase. But the problem is that once we have reached that phase, our job and other aspects of our lives suffer. People who experience chronic burnout have a 26% to 35% higher risk of early mortality (mortality under the age of 45) and are three times more likely to have an increased risk of experiencing future depression, and coronary heart disease. Also, the chance of their developing type 2 diabetes rises by 200 percent[29]. Burnout should not be taken lightly by you or the organizational leadership. So, what can we do to prevent this workplace phenomenon and avoid its severe complications?

While burnout is becoming increasingly prevalent in workplaces, it should be noted that it can often be confused with depression. Before I was diagnosed with bipolar disorder, there were consecutive days that I was ultimately withdrawn. I would just lay in bed, eating food and watching T.V. My usual drive to get up and get everything under the sun accomplished was utterly non-existent. My family knew these days well and often would just lay

[28] Burn-out an "occupational phenomenon": International Classification of Diseases, World Health Organization, May 28, 2019, https://www.who.int/news/item/28-05-2019-burn-out-an-occupational-phenomenon-international-classification-of-diseases, accessed March 21, 2023.

[29] Meng Li, The Danger of Burnout in the Workplace, The Ohio State University Fisher College of Business, August 5, 2020, https://fisher.osu.edu/blogs/leadreadtoday/danger-burnout-workplace.

with me for support. I would call out of work with some made-up excuse because I didn't quite know what was wrong with me, but I knew my workplace was the last place I wanted to be. In my head, I was burned out and just needed a break. Then, out of nowhere, I would suddenly return to my usual over-productive, high-on-life self. I would go back to the job I loved. I was not experiencing any of the phases of burnout. My work environment was not toxic, I wasn't feeling overwhelmed, and I was getting the support I needed. However, because I was not aware of the symptoms of depression, I assumed I was burned out. Remember, your workplace solely triggers burnout, according to WHO, so before you declare you are burned out, speak with a medical professional to confirm your diagnosis so you are correctly treated.

Many of you are reading this book because you saw "burnout" in the title, and you want to know what you can do to either stop being burned out or how to prevent it from taking you or your team. So, the first step in addressing burnout is identifying the common characteristics of people likely to burn out at work.

The Anxious Achiever

The Anxious Achiever is not a scientific term or clinical diagnosis but was coined by Morra Aarons-Mele, who hosts a podcast by the same name. The term is used to describe individuals who experience high anxiety levels while striving for success or achievement. These individuals may have perfectionistic tendencies, set high expectations for themselves, and experience anxiety or stress when they feel they are falling short of their goals. They may also experience imposter syndrome, a feeling of being a fraud despite their accomplishments.

Anxious achievers may push themselves to work harder and longer and feel guilty or ashamed when taking breaks or time off. They may also struggle with anxiety-related symptoms, such as racing thoughts and insomnia, or physical symptoms, like headaches or stomach problems. While striving for success can be positive and motivating, excessive anxiety and stress can negatively impact an individual's well-being, productivity, and relationships, making them likely to experience burnout.

The High Achiever

Maybe everyone thinks they are High Achievers in the workplace, but I've worked in H.R. for many years, and believe me, there are levels to performance in each organization. High Achievers do not tend to be motivated by money. Instead, they are driven by exceeding expectations. They also deal with overcommitment to their organizations, leading to difficulty delegating tasks to others. Additionally, many High Achievers tend to prioritize work over their personal lives, resulting in a lack of work-life balance. Chronic stress is also an issue for high achievers due to the constant pressure they put on themselves to perform at the highest level. Once the High Achiever senses that their work motivations are not being fulfilled, then they begin to transition into the phases of burnout. If the High Achiever reaches the final phases of burnout, the organization suffers since High Achievers can "provide 400% more productivity than an average employee." [30]

The Impersonator Achiever

Earlier, I discussed the concept of "fake it till you make it," but faking it at work can be exhausting and eventually lead to burnout. There are several reasons why someone may be faking it at work. As already mentioned, the person may be masking part of their

[30] Dr. Ruth Gotian, How to Attract, Retain, and Lead High Achievers, Forbes Magazine, June 29, 2020, https://www.forbes.com/sites/ruthgotian/2020/06/29/how-to-attract-retain-and-lead-high-achievers/?sh=349265810437.

identity to conform to corporate culture. Or, they may have embellished their skill set to get a job. Maybe, they are faking that they can handle the stresses of their jobs. Whatever the case, they can only fake it for so long. Perhaps they finally make it, meaning they achieve the desired results, but they are likely to burn out before that happens.

I felt like an imposter when I moved from the southern United States to New York City. All the confidence I had gained working in corporate America in the south had flown out of the window. I was paranoid about my accent, having a degree from UCLA (Unknown College in Lower Alabama), and even my southern hospitality (no one seemed to be smiling back at me as I walked down the street). When I started my new job, I immediately shed my natural southern persona in exchange for a more aggressive New York City persona. On my way to work, I would listen to accent elimination exercises and practice the common phrases I would hear New Yorkers say. I spent more time trying to be someone I wasn't instead of growing into the person I was meant to be.

One day, I realized how exhausting it was to be inauthentic. I also realized that there was nothing wrong with who I was. Outside of work, my southern personality and charm had gained the attention of my neighbors and friends. They were beginning to lean on me for their personal and work challenges because they knew I would respond in a kind, gentle manner (don't get me wrong, New Yorkers are kind and gentle, but just in their unique fashion). Slowly, I began to shed my fake persona and let the real me shine at work, and it worked, especially as it related to connecting with the other employees. Just by being me, I was able to gain their trust. I became credible in their eyes and their union reps, and, most importantly, I was able to spend more time growing as an H.R. professional and leader rather than burning myself out trying to be someone I wasn't.

The Perfect Achiever

You are probably wondering about the difference between the High Achiever and the Perfect Achiever. Let me explain. High achievers aim to exceed expectations and love innovation and personal development. Once they have reached their goals, they feel satisfied and accomplished. The Perfect Achiever rarely reaches a sense of satisfaction and accomplishment. Even when they are told that they performed well, the Perfect Achiever is critical of their work and focuses on everything they could have done differently or what went wrong in the process. I have worked under a perfectionist before. I remember spending hours editing company-wide emails with them, nitpicking every word and phrase, then going back and changing the email back to its original message. Their perfectionist attitude not only had the potential to burn them out, as they were constantly spinning their wheels and not getting anywhere but also led me to burn myself out.

The People Pleaser Achiever

No, is a complete sentence, but the People Pleaser doesn't know that. They want everyone around them to rely on them for everything. They enjoy doing "invisible tasks." We know they will take notes or order a dozen lunches for meetings when no one else volunteers. If there is a conflict or a difference of opinions, they will be adamant to remain neutral so as not to make anyone displeased with them. While this sounds like a "safe" way to work with others, it can come to the detriment of those who engage in this behavior. People pleasing can lead to being overwhelmed because they have difficulty saying "no." It can also become an obstacle to being able to contribute your actual value at work. For instance, why are you even here if you keep your opinions to yourself? You were hired for your knowledge and expertise. If you don't feel comfortable sharing those opinions because you are afraid you may ruffle some feathers, you are not fulfilling your duties. You are just there to serve others (which you weren't hired to do). Eventually, you reach the burnout phase because you are taking on unnecessary tasks and responsibilities, have difficulties saying "no" and delegating, and are suppressing what you are capable of doing in your role.

Leaders who are people pleasers are a detriment to any work environment. I used to work for one of those too. This particular leader could have done better in resolving conflict amongst her team members, but she wanted to avoid ruffling any feathers. She did not advocate for us either when unrealistic expectations were asked of us by our business partners or if someone complained about the advice we gave them. Her leadership style of being the People Pleaser became exhausting for all of us, and we all ended up eventually feeling burned out, walking out of that job, and finding new opportunities.

As you can see, no matter what category you fall into, you risk either burning yourself out or risk your behaviors burning out others. If you do not fall into any of these categories, that does not mean you are not at risk for burnout. Specific demographics are at a higher risk for burnout than others due to both workplace and non-workplace factors. For instance, a recent report[31] from Leanin.org, in partnership with McKinsey, revealed that women are "switching jobs at a higher rate than ever." The report cites the reasons being the underrepresentation in leadership, especially for women of color, experiencing microaggressions that "undermine their authority," having to spend unpaid time on DEI and well-being work that is not recognized, and the lack of flexibility in working hours. Women have to work harder than

---

[31] Women in the Workplace 2022, LeanIn.org, October 18, 2022, https://www.mckinsey.com/featured-insights/diversity-and-inclusion/women-in-the-workplace, accessed March 21, 2023.

men but receive significantly lower outcomes. This disparity leads to burnout, stress, and anxiety. That's why the women that the LeanIn article refers to are saying, "enough" and exiting their current work environments.

I encourage anyone reading this book who is experiencing burnout or falls into one of the categories I described earlier to say "enough" as well. But, saying enough doesn't necessarily mean that your next action is now to up and quit your job. It means you should shift how you approach work to prevent burnout and protect your mental health. But how do you do that?

Let's ask the experts.

I spoke with Dr. Tamara Beckford, MD, MS, and E.R. doctor, the CEO of U.R. Caring Docs, a company that helps organizations reduce employee burnout through self-care workshops. Dr. Beckford told me she realized that most of her burnout was self-imposed. As a physician, she used to put off documenting her patient's records until she got home. That practice became a regular part of her day. When she realized that bringing work home was interfering with her ability to spend time with her child, she changed her approach. She began to make time during her regularly scheduled shift to document and stopped bringing charts home. If she didn't get to document all of her charts that same day, she was fine with completing the task the next day. Since she shifted her practice of intentionally completing all of her tasks at work rather than bringing work home, she now feels less burned out. Now, she is helping other physicians find ways to prevent their own mental exhaustion burnout, as her profession has been cited as one of the most prone to stress, anxiety, and burnout.

Key Takeaway

INTENTIONALITY

SCHEDULE YOUR ENTIRE DAY WITH
INTENTIONALITY. THERE IS A TIME AND A PLACE
FOR EVERYTHING. WORK SHOULD BE PERFORMED
DURING WORKING HOURS UNLESS IN EXTREME
CIRCUMSTANCES. BUT, TAKE NOTE. YOU SHOULD BE
THE ONE DETERMINING THE BOUNDARY BETWEEN
WORKING AND NON-WORKING HOURS. IF YOU FIND
COMPLETING WORK DURING NON-WORKING HOURS
BENEFICIAL TO YOUR MENTAL WELL-BEING, THAT IS
FINE. MAKE SURE, HOWEVER, COMPLETING THESE
TASKS DOES NOT INTERFERE WITH OTHER
ESSENTIAL THINGS IN YOUR LIFE, SUCH AS
SPENDING TIME WITH YOUR FAMILY

When I spoke with Morra Aarons-Mele about how to overcome the anxiety at work that often leads to burnout, she emphasized how awareness is vital. If your anxiety is becoming debilitating, your heart is racing, you are not sleeping well, you are having trouble concentrating, or people are giving you feedback that you are micromanaging, you should dive deeper into why you are feeling this way. What is triggering your anxiety? How are you reacting to those triggers, and are those reactions beneficial for my anxiety? Char Newell, Chief Corporate Life Coach at Your Healthy Reality, agrees with Aarons-Mele. Newell, and suggests that to prevent burnout, you should understand your limits, strengths, weaknesses, and emotional state to set realistic expectations for yourself. She also encourages noticing how you feel in different situations and what is causing those emotions. Are there certain people, tasks, or situations that consistently drain your energy or leave you feeling overwhelmed? Recognizing these triggers can help you take action, make changes, and set boundaries that could prevent burnout.

Key Takeaway
KNOW YOUR TRIGGERS

MANY OF US ARE OPERATING ON AUTOPILOT IN HOW WE OPERATE AT WORK. WE FAIL TO TAKE THE TIME TO PAUSE AND TUNE INTO OUR EMOTIONS IN DIFFERENT SITUATIONS. WHEN WE DO THAT, HOWEVER, WE CAN DETERMINE WHAT MAKES US FEEL ANXIOUS, OVERWORKED, UNHAPPY, AND UNMOTIVATED AND TAKE STEPS TO AVOID THESE TRIGGERS.

When I started my non-profit for Workplace Mental Wellness last year, I had no idea what I was doing. There was such a difference between managing a non-profit and a for-profit organization. I had no donors, employees, or volunteers, so by the time I launched the foundation, I was already over the idea. Nevertheless, I decided to host a fundraising gala just six months later. In a short period, several people contacted me wanting to volunteer, and I built a fantastic board of directors and advisors. However, the only thing I did with these new resources was to create the foundation website. Despite these people offering their talents, I didn't think to utilize them. Instead, I was determined to do everything myself, including organizing the gala. It is no surprise, therefore, that by the time the gala concluded, I was burned out. Although the gala was a success, I lacked the energy needed to keep the momentum going. I will be honest with you, the foundation could be doing more than it is currently doing, but I have not dipped into the support system offered to me.

I have spoken with countless women who have struggled with asking for help. This is a systemic issue as we are often told that to get ahead at work, we must be fiercely independent and not appear as "weak." For some reason, we have translated this to mean that we shouldn't ask for or need support. As women, we couldn't be more wrong. Men have been relying on support in the workplace and their homes to advance in their careers for years. Even the "bro culture" that is often referred to in the workplace is an extension of men relying on each other in and outside of the workplace for support and advancement (mixed in with a little misogyny and sexual harassment). Other demographics need to shed the assumption that asking for help or support is considered weak. Building a strong network of supporters can make a significant difference to your mental health.

Key Takeaway
BUILD A SUPPORT SYSTEM

NEEDING, ASKING FOR, AND ACCEPTING SUPPORT IS NOT A SIGN OF WEAKNESS. IT HELPS YOU TO BUILD RESILIENCE AND ENDURANCE. IF YOU SURROUND YOURSELF WITH PEOPLE WHO ARE ROOTING FOR YOUR SUCCESS, EXERTING POSITIVE ENERGY WILL GIVE YOU CANDID FEEDBACK OR CONTRIBUTE TO YOUR LIFE IN OTHER POSITIVE WAYS, YOU ARE LESS LIKELY TO EXPERIENCE BURNOUT

One of my professional monikers is "The Workplace Doctor." Someone started to refer to me as that because of my ability to diagnose workplace issues and provide successful solutions. However, in my roles as an H.R. professional, the lines are often blurred between diagnosing and providing solutions to workplace issues and people's personal lives. I guess you can call me an empath. I can feel the emotions of people around me deeply and believe it to be my responsibility to address their feelings whether those emotions concern me or not. Over the years, people have picked up on this and often unload their emotional baggage on me even in the workplace. And, for years, I was a willing recipient of this unloading. My main goal was for everyone around me to be happy, no matter the cost to my mental health. Since I've been doing a better job at protecting my mental health, I no longer allow people to unload their emotional baggage on me if I don't have the capacity to take it on. However, as an H.R. professional and organizational leader, setting these psychological boundaries can be very difficult to do. But, to avoid burnout, everyone should determine what their emotional boundaries are and try their best not to let anyone cross them.

I was speaking with LeMetia Smith, who holds a Ph.D. in Psychology, and she explained to me that taking on the emotional baggage of others by listening to their problems day in and day out can be especially draining. The stress associated with these interactions can lead to compassion fatigue, which over time can cause burnout. She went on to explain that it is important to establish and maintain healthy boundaries and know when your psychological safety net is threatened.

Key Takeaway

ESTABLISH EMOTIONAL BOURNDARIES

ESTABLISH CLEAR BOUNDARIES WITH PEOPLE AND STICK TO THEM. THIS MEANS LETTING OTHERS KNOW WHAT YOU ARE AND AREN'T COMFORTABLE WITH. SET BOUNDARIES AROUND HOW MUCH TIME YOU SPEND WITH SOMEONE, WHAT TOPICS ARE OFF-LIMITS, AND WHAT BEHAVIORS ARE UNACCEPTABLE

Christi Venable, Founder, and CEO of Smile Therapy Services, LLC, advises that people experiencing burnout should invest more in their well-being. One way you can achieve this is to take time off, even if it is just a few days, to reset and recharge.

Additionally, Venable suggests that self-care, such as getting enough sleep, eating healthy meals, and exercising regularly, can help with burnout. Self-care is essential for preventing burnout because it can help to reduce stress levels, increase self-confidence, and improve overall well-being. It can also help to provide a sense of clarity and balance. Regular self-care activities can help provide perspective and allow for reflection, which may help you identify the root causes of your burning out.

Key Takeaway

ENGAGE IN SELF-CARE

REGULAR SELF-CARE ACTIVITIES CAN PROVIDE A SENSE OF CONTROL AND A BREAK FROM THE DAILY GRIND. ADDITIONALLY, SELF-CARE CAN HELP PROVIDE MUCH-NEEDED MENTAL AND EMOTIONAL BREAKS FROM LIFE'S STRESSORS, WHICH CAN HELP PREVENT BURNOUT.

After reading this advice and guidance on preventing burnout in the workplace, do you feel like none of these scenarios apply to your current situation, yet you're still unhappy and unmotivated at work? For instance, you may have already set boundaries to balance your work and life. You may not be overworked and may have already been given the resources you need for success. Maybe you are being paid your value for the work you do. You may even have a supportive, compassionate manager who cares about your well-being. Yet, you still feel you need to be more motivated and happier at work. If this is the case, don't worry, you are not alone. I have been there before, and so have others.

Throughout my professional years, I have had several conversations with employees who are just not happy or motivated at work despite working in a positive and healthy workplace. I have learned that many people have entered careers because of the expectations of others, or they were chasing superficial things such as prestige, money, or maintaining a family tradition. I came from a family of educators, and at one point, I thought I would continue that tradition. So, while attending college, I worked as a substitute teacher for two years while taking classes at night. Those were some of the worst years of my life. Just like when I sold shoes, there was not anything toxic about the work environment; it was just me. That was not the career for me. I would later discover that I did love teaching but teaching adults, not children. So, if, after reading this chapter, you still feel hopeless about your future in your current job, you may be masking your unhappiness under the guise of burnout, but burnout may not be the source of your unhappiness.

The symptoms of burnout and unhappiness or stress from non-work-related issues are similar, so it is easier for many to blame their jobs for their chronic stress. To determine if you are experiencing work-related burnout or are chronically stressed due to non-work-related factors, here are some actions to consider:

- Evaluate if other factors in your life are causing you to stress such as unhealthy relationships, financial uncertainty, or being overwhelmed with home responsibilities.
- Reflect on why you entered your career or started your job in the first place. Were you motivated by passion or money, other people, or prestige?
- Determine whether you may have outgrown your career and that it may be time to pursue something new and exciting.

Exploring these questions may be difficult as you may conclude that you have been blaming everyone and everything else other than the fact you have invested a lot of time, energy, and money into a career or job that is not right for you, and it may be time to move on. Do not fret, though. In the next chapter, I will show you how you can plan your exit strategy from your current situation, whether you are dealing with burnout or are just unmotivated and unhappy with your current job or career.

Changing careers or jobs can feel like a crazy idea, but remember, the point of this book is to be crazy A.F. We are stepping outside of our comfort zone to find peace and happiness at work.

CHAPTER 11

EXITING HARM

As we conclude the third part of this book, we now know that in most workplaces worldwide, mental health is too often misunderstood, under-resourced, and deprioritized compared to physical health. People with mental health conditions are routinely stigmatized, discriminated against, and excluded. Widespread stigma creates a barrier. Some employers may be reluctant to hire people with mental health conditions, and some workers may hesitate to disclose or seek help because they fear negative career consequences.

Although employers have responded with initiatives like mental health days or weeks, four-day workweeks, and enhanced counseling benefits or apps, more is needed. Employees expect sustainable and mentally healthy workplaces, which requires taking on the real work of culture change. It is not enough to offer the latest apps or employ euphemisms such as "well-being" or "mental fitness." Employers must connect what they say to what they do. In the preceding chapters of this book, I have offered practical solutions for organizational leaders and individual contributors as guidance for going from being burned out, unmotivated, and unhappy to reclaiming their mental health at work. But I must admit that no matter how much you apply these tactics, you may still be working in a harmful environment. This discovery is not abnormal, as cultivating cultures of mental wellness in the workplace requires commitment and participation by both organizational leaders and you. Suppose your organization is unwilling to remove the barriers that stand in the way of your experiencing a healthy and positive work environment. Or they are unwilling to invest the time and resources to improve the situation. In that case, you may have to plan your exit strategy.

Once I discovered the career that I loved in human resources, I soon learned that no matter how passionate and committed I was to the organization, there always seemed to be some external, environmental factor that prohibited me from achieving job satisfaction and intrinsic motivation that I desired. For me, that was usually the result of poor leadership. After the cycle of going from rock star to rock bottom continued, mainly stemming from my work environment (and once due to a poor decision by me because of my undiagnosed mental illness), I began practicing the habit of planning my exit strategy as soon as I accepted a job offer. Now, I know that sounds crazy. But that's why I am writing this book. To succeed in our careers, we must be willing to do the unthinkable. We can no longer remain on auto-pilot. We must be intentional in creating the work-life harmony we deserve and desire.

As an H.R. professional, I have been given the privilege of having access to unpublished playbooks. What do I mean by that? Well, let me give you an example. I watch a lot of college football. I mean, a lot. If you have ever watched a college football game (and this may even happen in the N.F.L.), you may notice that on the sidelines the coaches will hold up big posters with these cryptic messages alerting the teams of their play calls. If you're a member of that team, you need to learn what these cryptic messages mean. The other team has posters of cryptic messages as well. The most successful teams spend countless hours watching films of their opposing teams past games to predict their strategies and plan accordingly. After completing the play, you will know whose cryptic message will succeed. Sometimes, you can predict what the other team will do by breaking the code of their message based on their past games.

Okay, enough about college football. Let me get to my point. Workplaces remind me a lot of college football. However, the winning record leans towards organizational leaders. Why? Because as workers, we need to spend more time focusing on how our leaders have played in the past and plan a strategy to beat them at their own game. When we show up unprepared, we get run over. In the end, we look at the scoreboard to see:

The Home Team (Your Workplace): 100
Visitors (Us): 0

That is called a blowout. Our workplaces tend to suck every piece of energy, knowledge, and value that we have to contribute. Yeah, we get paid for some of this, but oftentimes the energy we give is more than what we're paid for. Because we've poured everything we have into our workplaces and have not been rewarded with a safe, healthy, and positive work environment. You feel like you do not matter. You feel defeated. But, if you study the past performance of organizations and develop your own playbook and strategy, you don't have to feel that dreaded defeat when it's time to say goodbye, voluntarily or involuntarily. So, as someone who has seen their playbook and knows what those cryptic messages are on the sidelines, I am about to share everything your organization does not want you to know when it comes to reclaiming your mental health at work.

But first, let me just put this out there as well. It may seem like I am just talking to individual contributors right now. However, I have seen executives in the same situations I have described above. Because they are executives, the expectation is that they commit their lives to their companies. However, they, too, have felt burned out, stressed, overworked, and eventually unhappy in their jobs. For instance, recently, the Prime Minister of New Zealand, Jacinda Arden, who served in her leadership position for over five and a half years, announced that she was stepping down because she "no longer had enough left in her tank." She went on to say, "I'm leaving because with such a privileged role comes responsibility – the responsibility to know when you are the right person to lead and also when you are not. I know what this job takes. It's that simple."[32] Bravo, Jacinda, bravo! Not many people in the workplace, let alone leaders, know when their time to leave has come.

It takes courage to know when you no longer have "enough in your tank" or that you are feeling mentally exhausted, overwhelmed, and unappreciated. It takes courage to know that when you have reached that point, you are not doing yourself or others justice. And it takes courage to know that even when you have put your best foot forward, sometimes the cards (those cryptic cards) are just stacked against you. So, let's not wait until your mental health is on the line. That is dangerous and irresponsible. It is akin to feeling heart palpitations squeezing in your left arm, and not going to the emergency room. So, no matter your role, sit up and pay attention. Let's be proactive with planning for your mental and physical well-being, psychological safety, and financial security.

As an H.R. professional, I have learned what those cryptic messages in the workplace mean and how employees have missed these messages that have been hiding in plain sight. Understanding what these cryptic messages mean allows you to see the warning signs that it may be time to start planning your exit strategy.

---

[32] Tess McClure, Jacinda Arden Resigns as Prime Minister of New Zealand, The Guardian, January 18, 2023, https://www.theguardian.com/world/2023/jan/19/jacinda-ardern-resigns-as-prime-minister-of-new-zealand.

These messages are categorized as CAUTION or RED FLAG.

⚠ **The caution symbol** means that you should pause and get clarity on any underlying circumstances that could quickly be resolved through a conversation with your manager or someone else in the organization. We all tend to "make up stories in our heads." Sometimes, we are right about being sent a message that we are no longer welcome at our jobs, but sometimes we have misinterpreted what is going on.

⚑ **The flag symbol** means "red flag" – you are definitely at risk for your mental well-being being disrupted because your workplace is engaging in harmful, toxic behaviors. If you encounter any of these behaviors, you should immediately start executing your exit strategy that we will discuss later.

Now that you have the key, let's begin by identifying the 20 cryptic messages that it may be time to execute your exit strategy.

⚠ During your performance review, you hear for the first time that you are not meeting expectations. An additional sign is that there is no qualitative or quantitative data to back up the assessment. There are typically two reasons why this happens: 1) You have a manager that sucks or is too lazy to give immediate feedback, or 2) Unexpected negative feedback is the beginning of the process of your organization preparing its documentation to separate you from the company.

⚠ You start being removed from essential projects and meetings with no explanation. This caution is because 1) You are not meeting performance expectations; or 2) Once again, this is part of the process of your organization preparing to separate you from the company.

⚠️ You are the only person in your organization or leadership team from your demographic, i.e., the only Black person, the only woman, etc. This sign could indicate that you are a token for the organization, which is a performative way to show commitment to D.E.I. efforts.

⚠️ You work in a position where remote work, at least on a hybrid basis, is possible, but not allowed. This sign indicates that your organization does not value work-life harmony, which promotes mental well-being, or they have trust issues. All relationships should be based on trust.

⚠️ Discussions about mental health are discouraged, and E.A.P. is the only resource available.

⚠️ Your organization is using phrases like "culture fit." I believe that shoes fit, not humans. Culture should be like a puzzle, not a constant shape.

⚠️ Your manager or company stalks your social media, and you are reprehended for speaking the truth about your current work environment or the workplace in general.

⚠️ You are discouraged from pursuing outside passions or "side hustles."

⚠️ Microaggressions are rampant, and people think they are funny rather than offensive.

🚩 Your manager has a history of bullying people and fueling toxicity. They have been reported to H.R. and upper management numerous times, but nothing has happened.

When you report toxic behaviors in your workplace, your performance comes under fire.

Your organization centers its holidays, observances, and celebrations around one nationality, race, or religion. This sign could signal that while your organization may have representation, its culture is not welcoming and inclusive of diverse representation.

You are allotted sick or vacation days but have difficulty getting approval, or some policies penalize you for taking them. For instance, you are allotted twelve sick days a year, but another policy states how often you are actually allowed to take or else face being written up. These are usually under the guise of Time and Attendance policies.

You feel like you need to "code switch" at work. If you don't know what code-switching means, it's when you feel the need to change the way you speak, appear, behave, or express yourself at work for fear of discomforting others or not "fitting in" to the culture.

Your psychological safety is always at risk. Psychological safety can be described as "the belief that you won't be punished or humiliated for speaking up with ideas, questions, concerns, or mistakes."[33]

You feel like an imposter in your workplace. Feeling like an imposter means that you doubt that your background, education,

[33] What Is Psychological Safety at Work? How Leaders Can Build Psychologically Safe Workplaces, Center for Creative Leadership, December 15, 2022, https://www.ccl.org/articles/leading-effectively-articles/what-is-psychological-safety-at-work/, accessed on March 20, 2023.

past work experiences, and accomplishments are good enough for your organization. You have received no validation from your leadership team that you are adding value and are appreciated.

Your credibility is questioned. Despite your education, knowledge, and experience, your manager feels the need to constantly validate your knowledge.

Your manager invites H.R. whenever they meet with you. Again, this means they are planning your exit and want to ensure all their ducks are in a row.

You are placed on a Performance Improvement Plan (P.I.P.). These plans are given out under the guise that you have a certain amount of time to improve your performance, or you'll be terminated. Your manager and H.R. will say they want you to succeed, but it is just a C.Y.A. tactic.

You are being targeted or treated differently from others on your team or organization for engaging in the same behavior or performing at the same level. Your mistakes are called out, but your colleagues' errors are not. When you bring this disparity to the offender's attention, they respond, "We're not discussing them. We're discussing you." Or "How do you know we haven't had the same conversation with [the other offenders]?"

*****

Did any of these cryptic messages resonate with you? I am almost sure at least one did. I've placed these cryptic messages in no particular order, and there is no formula for how many of these you should "check off" before you "check out." However, I always advise people to follow their gut. You know when something is off in your workplace. When you feel in the pit of your stomach that you are no longer welcome, it is time to take action. These cryptic messages are unspoken signs that your organization no longer wants you around, and staying in a toxic work environment can cause unbelievable harm. Remember how I shared with you that my husband remained in a toxic work environment even after he started to experience both physical and mental symptoms of extreme stress? The result was that the anxiety that developed out of that situation, which wasn't there before, never went away. And he left the career that he loved and never returned. We should never let one leader, workplace, or experience stop us from doing what we love. We deserve better than that. We deserve to protect our mental health AND our wealth.

Your ultimate exit strategy may look different from mine. Still, this strategy has worked for me to transition from one job to another without wide gaps in income all while maintaining my mental health and dignity.

The Exit Strategy

Document, document, document!

I document everything from the very first day I start a job to my very last day. I document the horrible things my boss has said or done and my accomplishments. I also include any volunteer work, such as sitting on committees and hosting and attending company-sponsored events. Often, we wait until we realize some of those cryptic messages are happening before we begin to document them, and our memory will only let us go back so far. Additionally, when our brain is in "fight or flight" mode, we tend to only focus on what others are doing to us rather than what we have done for them. You may not even need this but hold onto that folder of documentation. Ensure you are keeping your documentation on a non- company-owned device. You never know when your access may be cut off. Then, you are screwed.

Leverage the Power of LinkedIn

Most people need to realize LinkedIn's power and use it to their advantage. I have been on the platform for ten years. I was among the first people to actively use it not to find a job but to share my workplace expertise. At that time, I wrote a lot about workplace law. The next thing I knew, I started receiving messages from recruiters all over with attractive opportunities. I even got my first professorship at a prestigious university without even applying. All in all, I got 10 jobs through LinkedIn without going through the application process. These actions started my "side hustle" career, but more on that later.

Have you ever wondered why you never got a call about a job you applied to when your resumè was perfect for the opportunity? It is because recruiters HATE going through applicant tracking systems (A.T.S.). They can receive thousands of applications. Even when you use filters, the numbers are ridiculous. They would much rather already have someone in mind for the position. Why can't that be you? I want to go into more detail about leveraging your LinkedIn profile, but the point is to DO IT. You will thank me later. For the best tips for gaining attraction to your LinkedIn profile, follow Lakrisha Davis or buy Simone E. Morris' book, *52 Tips for Owning Your Career.*[34]

Here are some tips for proactively leveraging LinkedIn:
- Keep your profile updated. Many organizations have an option for you to use just your LinkedIn profile to apply for a job instead of uploading a resume. But have that resume ready, as well.
- Turn on LinkedIn notifications that will alert you of available job opportunities you may be interested in pursuing.

---

[34] Simone E. Morris, 52 Tips for Owning Your Career, Second Edition, Simone Morris Enterprises, November 14, 2022.

- If there is a particular company you are interested in working with, follow the key players in that company. Not the C.E.O., per se, but someone that leads the department that you would work in and their recruiters. Engage in their posts. Let them know you exist. **Caution:** don't become annoying when engaging with them (but I will talk about that next).
- Actively post on LinkedIn. Becoming an active and respected part of your profession is essential. Do not just pop up out of nowhere when you lose or leave your job and start posting. Becoming a well-respected member of your profession is critical to transition easily from one job to another. However, as you post, do not tag the same people in every single post, every single day, to get their attention. Some people do that to me, and it becomes annoying, quite frankly. Tag them on meaningful posts that demonstrate your thought leadership in your profession.

I cannot stress enough how important it is to leverage the power of LinkedIn. If you are spending more time on other social media networks, stop now and spend that time on LinkedIn. Additionally, your workplace does not own your LinkedIn profile. I have seen too many people make the mistake of only promoting their organization's brand but failing to promote their own. You are a brand! What happens when that organization lays you off or you exit for some other reason? Your followers know nothing about you other than you are an ex-[X.Y.Z. Company]. You are under no obligation to promote your organization's brand.

Think about this. As a business owner, I always get offers from marketing companies proposing to create content for my company. They propose charging me thousands of dollars per month without guarantee of converting any leads to clients. Each time you promote your organization's brand to your followers, imagine the monetary value that it brings them, especially if you have a large following. I am not discouraging you from bragging about your job or company, posting a position, or sharing your organization's accomplishments. I am challenging you to think about this: whose dreams are you making come true? Yours or theirs? Leveraging LinkedIn can be a game changer and saves you a ton of time not looking for a job when the time comes but possibly being presented with a tremendous opportunity even before you need to.

Now, here is where the real fun comes in.
Proactively Transitioning Out of Your Workplace

Whether you see that the cryptic messages or the signs are overt, or you finally understand that no job is permanent (the days of working thirty years in one place and then retiring are over), you must plan your exit strategy. If you have not been lucky enough for a new job to find you before you find one, and you are desperate to exit, these next steps are for you.

Here are a couple of things I want you to consider.

> Has illegal conduct in the workplace occurred? Meaning, have you been unlawfully discriminated against, harassed, or retaliated against?

> If the answer is "yes," have you reported the illegal behavior to H.R.? I know many of you do not trust H.R., but there are some good ones out there (like me). But, in some instances, even H.R. can't help you. But we want to!

> If the answer is "yes," then have you reported the illegal behavior to someone in upper management? If not, give it a shot. Go as high as you can go. Do not hesitate to inform the C.E.O., if you need to. I will tell you why in a little bit.

> Lastly, have you cross-checked your perception with someone close to the situation? If you have been on the receiving end of some of those cryptic messages, then it is likely other people have noticed what is going on as well.

Hopefully, you have someone you can confide in at work to validate what you believe you are experiencing.

The last checkpoint is vital because many people suffer from Previous Traumatic Workplace Toxicity Disorder (P.T.W.T.D.) from a previous toxic workplace. P.T.W.T.D. is not a medical definition, but it should be. Due to bad experiences at past workplaces, some people become overly paranoid about their current work environment. They have been abused and harmed for so long and in so many workplaces that constructive feedback can be perceived as aggression when it is not. Again, this is an example of what happens when we do not seek treatment for our mental health when we have been harmed.

Assuming you are not suffering from P.T.W.T.D. and have answered "yes" to the first three questions, it is time to move on to the next step.

Know Your Workplace Rights

If you work in a toxic environment, you have probably already developed chronic stress, anxiety, or other severe mental or physical symptoms. If this is the case, you need to take some time off to get treatment *and* plot your next move. There are two ways to get job-protected time off to protect your mental health in the United States:

1) FMLA
If you've worked for your current company for 1250 hours in the previous 12 months or year, you are entitled to 12 weeks of job-protected, unpaid leave under the Family Medical Leave Act (FMLA). You can get 26 weeks if you are a service member or a military caregiver. All you need to do is get a doctor to certify that you have been diagnosed with a severe medical condition, and chronic stress and anxiety are considered serious medical conditions. The leave is unpaid, but your employer may have a

policy where you can use your P.T.O. to be paid for this time off, or you may eligible for short term disability through your State.

2) A.D.A.

Unlike the FMLA, you are entitled to rights under the Americans with Disabilities Act (A.D.A.) from the moment you apply for a job. This means that you are entitled to a workplace accommodation if you have a disability or a perceived disability. Without going into the ins and outs of the act, chronic stress, anxiety, and depression brought on by working in a toxic workplace can be considered a disability under the A.D.A. If your work-related medical condition is considered a disability under the A.D.A., you can ask for unpaid time off as a reasonable accommodation. Suppose you are eligible for FMLA and need more than 12 weeks. In that case, you may be eligible for additional time by asking for reasonable accommodation for more time off under the A.D.A.

For more information about these two U.S. workplace laws, I dive deeper into this in my book *You Can't Do That at Work*.

Using Your Time Off Wisely

Now that you are away from your toxic work environment, use this time wisely. You have exhausted all your options internally, and your workplace will not respond appropriately. It is time to think about what comes next. The goal is not to return to your toxic workplace but to transition to something bigger, better, and healthier. Hopefully, you have taken my advice and have already started leveraging LinkedIn. Therefore, you can use this time to reach out directly to recruiters. Some people may choose to use this time to start their own business. But you certainly want to use this time to begin holding your company accountable for not providing a positive, healthy, and psychologically safe work environment for you.

You have leverage now that you are on medical leave due to your toxic work environment. The ball is in your court. Your company should have responded appropriately. Begin with pulling out that folder of documentation that I suggested you keep. Use this documentation to write a formal letter to H.R. and all the powers that may be involved about your experience working for them. Your letter should entail the following:

- The details about the specific behaviors that caused your medical condition. Go into the who, the what, the when, and the where.
- If others were treated differently, i.e., better, then definitely emphasize that point because that is where the unlawfulness element comes in, especially if the people treated better are outside your demographic. This disparity is called disparate treatment.
- State why it would cause further harm for you to return to your workplace after your leave. If your medical provider is willing to justify this, have them write a letter to supplement yours.
- Tell your employer what you need (monetary settlement) for a seamless transition out of the organization. This indicates that you are willing to leave without pursuing any legal action.
- Give them a timeframe to respond before you pursue your next steps.

Brace yourself for their next move. They will deny all allegations that you have stated in your letter. Reading or hearing their response will be jarring, so make sure you have a full support system behind you and your mental health provider available to help you manage this process without causing more harm to your mental health. Let me tell you this. Few organizations will say, "We've substantiated all of your claims, and here is your payout." Your best-case scenario is that they substantiate your claims, remove the threat(s), and you return to a healthy environment. But remember, you have already shot these allegations up the chain of command, and they have denied or have not responded at this point. So, they will likely still deny, deny, deny.

Even if they substantiate your allegations, they may say that their conduct was not unlawful. They may be right. In the U.S., you can be a jerk at work under federal workplace laws. That means that if the culture sucks for everyone, they can get away with it. However, if you make enough noise, they usually want you to just take the pay and go away.

If they have been giving you cryptic messages that they want you out of there, they will respond by denying the allegations but will offer you some counter-settlement. How much they offer will depend on several factors, such as:

- how long you've been with the company
- your current total rewards package
- the severity of your claims
- what they have offered others in the past

I have been authorized to approve settlements from one month of pay to two years, plus continued medical benefits. If they do not offer you anything and tell you your job is waiting for you upon your return, you still have a couple of options:

- seek out the advice of an attorney
- file a claim with the E.E.O.C. or your State's agency that handles workplace rights

(Again, for more information about this process, check out my book, *You Can't Do That at Work!*)

If executed right, there is a strong probability that you will not only get time off work to repair the harm caused to your mental health by working in the toxic work environment, but you will also walk away with money to take more time off of work, start your own business, or to pay off bills while you start the transition into a new job.

Let me make one thing clear. Getting involved in settlement talks and lawsuits can harm your mental health more than you can imagine. You will hear things about yourself and your work performance that you have never heard before. Coworkers you thought were your friends and confidants may turn their backs on you. Do not take it personally. They are just not prepared for the retaliation that will likely ensue. Pursuing or threatening legal action should be the absolute last consideration. Leveraging your LinkedIn profile so that you can easily transition into another job or start a side hustle that you pursue full-time should be your first go-to. While it feels good to "make 'em pay" for their actions, that feeling does not last long.

A Note to Organizational Leaders

Can I be honest with you? I hate that I have to share the inside scoop on how employees can use the legal system to transition out of your organization. I would much rather spend my time advising you on how to protect the mental health of your workforce by cultivating cultures of mental wellness instead. If you have been engaging in any of the cryptic ways I described earlier to exit an employee out of your organization, I urge you to stop now.

There is no need for that. Instead, I encourage you to ask yourself:

- Why am I engaging in these underhanded tactics?
- Is there any reason I can't be honest with the employee about their performance or my perception of them?
- Are my biases informing my actions?
- Am I openly listening to the advice of my H.R. partner?
- Why should someone undergo these measures just so they can feel valued, respected, and treated equitably at work?
- What can I do instead?

The Side Hustle

Another part of your exit strategy to ensure the continuation of financial wellness is to start a "side hustle." Beginning a side hustle doesn't have to be time-consuming or stressful but having that side gig can be a game changer should you separate from your workplace. When I started "side hustling," not only was I able to begin to solidify financial security for my family, but I also felt a sense of empowerment and internal satisfaction. I began by teaching college classes at night and on weekends. Becoming a college professor added to my credibility as a thought leader and expert in my field, leading to consulting gigs and speaking engagements. I also wrote my first book as a "side hustle." A side hustle can come in different ways for different people. You can be a graphic designer, a freelance writer, or sell used clothes online. It doesn't matter.

I know you are probably thinking, "Natasha, I'm already burned out and don't have enough hours in my day for my regular job. How am I supposed to make time for another job!" That's the point. Whatever side hustle you engage in should not feel like a "job." It should be something that brings you self-satisfaction, motivation, and a feeling of self-worth. When I taught a class on Saturdays from 9-5 in addition to working a full-time job, I looked forward to it. I was the C.E.O. of that classroom. I decided what we would talk about, what I would teach, and how that day would be spent. I loved getting to know and mentoring my students, many of whom I still have close relationships with today. Unlike my full-time job at the time, I did not dread going to my side job. So, as you determine what side hustle is right for you, think about what will bring you that satisfaction. Entering the side hustle world will involve sacrifices, such as using your vacation days, weekends, and lunch breaks. However, if you ever start to feel overwhelmed, take a step back. That is okay! You can always start again when the time is right.

At the beginning of this book, I told you crazy is a verb, not a noun. Now you know why. What I've described using the

F.A.M.E. model are things that most of you may not have EVER thought about doing and still fear doing, even though some of these things may be resonating too well with you now. But have no fear. The final section of this book will provide you with the tools you need to be Crazy A.F. That is, Crazy And Fearless! Several years ago, Sheryl Sandberg wrote a book called *Lean In* and subsequently built an online community around her mission of "help[ing] women achieve their ambitions and work to create an equal world."[35] While the book's aim is for women to achieve workplace goals by talking "openly about the challenges *women* face [at work]," Sandberg's message and my work in advocating for workplace mental wellness share some of the same objectives. But there is one stark contrast. *Lean In* asks women to "lean" into the constructs of inequitable systems and find ways to navigate them rather than dismantle or abandon them as I encourage those facing mental health challenges to do. If you are committed to reclaiming your mental health at work, you must also be committed to pushing past your comfort zone and be prepared to lean out of toxic, unhealthy, and unsafe workplaces. Instead, you should lean into protecting your mental health. If you are anything like me and struggle with prioritizing your well-being, this concept may feel unfamiliar, frightening, yet exciting. But isn't that what facing your fears is all about? Are you ready for the last part of your journey? Let's get ready to get Crazy and Fearless.

---

[35] Sheryl Sandberg and Elisa Donovan et al., Lean In, Deckle Edge, March 2013.

PART IV

Crazy
&
FEARLESS

"

Media mogul Oprah Winfrey didn't always live the glamorous life that we see portrayed online today. During her childhood years, she was molested by several family members, abandoned by her mother, and witnessed domestic violence in her home. Before achieving success, she dealt with being rejected as a news anchor. However, despite these adversities during her lifetime that ultimately impacted her mental health, Oprah relentlessly pursued her dreams. She has fearlessly broken gender and racial ceilings in the media industry and continues to use her influence to shed light and break the stigma of mental illness across the globe.

CHAPTER 12

IN THE PURSUIT OF HAPPINESS

You have made it to Part IV, the final section of this book. Congratulations! Up to this point, you have been taken on a journey of learning about the experiences of those living with mental health conditions, how our workplaces have contributed to the mental health crisis, and the importance of protecting and advocating for your mental health. In this final portion, I will equip you with a roadmap for becoming crazy and fearless. I realize that some of the things I have suggested in this book have been frightening to think about implementing, especially when we tackled the F.A.M.E. framework.

Can I admit something to you? Sometimes it's just easier to keep to the status quo. Shoot, I was diagnosed with a mental illness over the age of forty. With the exception of a couple of dangerous manic episodes, mental illness had not negatively impacted my life. I had achieved things beyond my imagination. Why re-evaluate and disrupt my life now? Why shift my career to becoming essentially a full-time mental health advocate? Because the decisions I make now do not just affect me but affect the future. I want my kids, my nieces, and nephews, your kids, and our future grandkids, to live in an equitable world where they can be good people, and not feel shame for things beyond their control. So, as we move forward through the final journey of this book, let's unmask ourselves and reflect on what this world has the potential to be if we all could just be free to live fearlessly.

It took a mental health crisis for me to realize just how much I tied my identity to my profession. Without my profession, I felt worthless. I know that sounds strange, but it was my truth. Growing up as a Black woman in the southern United States, there was a lot of judgment about you based on your level of education. I was part of an elite group of Black people who had two college-educated parents. So, getting a college degree and then obtaining a law degree completed me. It's a little embarrassing to admit this, but I treasured my professional success more than being a wife or mother at times or any other positive attributes that I held.

I later learned that I was not alone in not knowing who I was without my professional success. There is a term for this phenomenon called "enmeshment." Enmeshment describes when "the boundaries between people become blurred and individual identities lose importance[36]. Enmeshment prevents the development of a stable, independent sense of self." I had not enmeshed with another person, but with my career. According to psychologist Janna Koretz, people working in high-pressure fields spend so much time attached to their work that they "displace" other things that they identify with. Koretz also adds that "our identities highly influence how we present ourselves." For me, I took pride in making public announcements that I was traveling internationally for a speaking engagement or had just signed on a new client. When the pandemic put those things on hold, I completely lost my identity because those things were enmeshed with who I was as a person.

---

[36] Janna Koretz, What Happens When Your Career Becomes Your Whole Identity, Harvard Business Review, December 26, 2019, https://hbr.org/2019/12/what-happens-when-your-career-becomes-your-whole-identity.

In the pursuit of happiness at work and in life, we often make the mistake of relying on others to give us the feeling of purpose that we so eagerly desire. Truth is, having strong interpersonal connections and a support system is part of that formula, but the common denominator is us. What I mean by this is for us to be happy at work and in our careers, there is a strong reliance on our ability to show up authentically and be fearlessly confident in our abilities. Remember how I explained the concept of leaning into ourselves in the previous section? This chapter will provide you with guidance on how you can do that. Before we can lean into others, we must lean into ourselves.

Lean Into Acceptance

One of the first steps to reclaiming your mental health at work is to reclaim your identity and become fearlessly, authentically you. Accepting who we authentically are can be frightening. After I was discharged from the mental health facility, it took time to discover who I was as a person, not just as a professional. I remembered that I used to be a dancer growing up and still loved it. I even found a niche for interior design and redecorated our entire home. And, of course, I had to remind myself of my most important title, being a wife and mom. What I discovered during that process was that I thought that other people's admiration of me was solely based on my professional accomplishments. But I was wrong. The people close to me saw and were proud of me for so many other things. Now that my career is back in full swing, I still have to be reminded that I am more than my work. And I want to remind you of that as well.

Workplaces can also be vessels in which we lose our identities. In the last part of the book, I wrote about how I felt the need to "code switch" when I first moved to New York as I was paranoid about how my southern accent would be perceived. The same is true for many people in marginalized groups or who believe they are misfits within their organizations. We have been programmed to a certain standard of "professionalism" by our outer appearance, the way we talk, and how we think. Anything perceived outside of the corporate norm is unacceptable and we have gone through great deals to shed our authentic identities to mitigate being rejected by our workplaces. When people ask me what it means to be psychologically safe at work, one of the key aspects of psychological safety is the ability to be authentically me.

The pandemic allowed many of us to blur the lines between our professional and personal lives which historically had a strong boundary between the two. I remember when Facebook became a thing, I would get chastised by so many people because they knew I had high career goals, but instead I chose to share intimate, vulnerable moments of my life on the platform. We are talking about sharing a picture of having a glass of wine at dinner, folks! But we are programmed that if you have certain career goals, you should not show up as "human." You needed to be some sort of robot that always wears business attire and never has fun. And, most definitely, does not have personal issues.

I will never forget when my kindergarten teacher invited me and one of her other favorite students to her wedding. It took me the longest time to get over imagining her having a boyfriend. Then, at the wedding, she kissed him! Teachers are not supposed to kiss! She danced and had fun that night too. I never looked at her the same way. She was no longer "Miss Smith," she was just a regular person. Now, things have changed. We are no longer suit-wearing, straight-faced, robots with no personal lives at work. During the pandemic, our workplaces were invited into our homes and our colleagues saw all the intimate, personal things about us. Now they know we have children, spouses, dogs, and cats. Our hair is curly, straight, pink, and blue. And yes, we have problems too.

Authenticity and acceptance of who we are, flaws and all, in the workplace is a critical component for our mental health at work. It will take a collective effort to reset the definition of professionalism, but it will take individual courage to show up fearlessly and authentically you. Why is being fearless and authentic at work so important, and why is it so hard to do?

There are several answers to that question but for each individual, the answer is different. Some people are afraid to be authentic at work because no one else there shares their background, culture, or physical attributes. Some are ashamed that they may have gotten to where they are unconventional. Others are afraid to be authentic because they have spent so much time being who others want them to be that they have forgotten who they genuinely are. The latter has caused people to pursue superficial things rather than what brought them into their careers anyway. I wanted to be a labor and employment law attorney because my passion was removing illegal obstacles people faced that kept them from advancing in their professions. However, when I interned in an in-house legal department in corporate America during law school, I noticed immediately that the most admired people were not those that were pouring their hearts into their jobs, but those who had managed to climb the corporate ladder, by any means necessary. Slowly, but surely, even after I graduated from law school, my passion changed. Instead of wanting to remove those barriers, I wanted to become the Vice President. As I was attempting to achieve that title, I lost not only my genuine passion along the way, but there were other parts of me that I lost along the way as well.

When I started to share my bipolar disorder diagnosis, people kept telling me I was brave. At first, I accepted those phrases as compliments, but then I started to think, why am I being considered brave just by sharing my whole self? When I think of someone being brave, I think of them being confronted with an uncomfortable situation, yet still going through with it. I'm afraid of heights, for example, so when I go on roller coasters with my thrill-seeking daughter, I am brave. When I walk alone along the streets of New York City, I am brave. One time while visiting Florida, I held an alligator. I was brave. And, for me, admitting when I am not okay, is being brave. But I don't think telling people that I have a medical condition should be considered brave. It is just being fearlessly, authentically me.

Every single piece of who I am has gotten me to where I am today. I have embraced that certain aspects of my identity are not typically accepted by society. This has been crucial to my journey to not just becoming successful (by my definition) but has led me to true happiness and fulfillment in life and in my career. I do not exhaust myself by living my life as if I am playing multiple roles in a Broadway play, always having to change costumes, accents, and personas. I am Natasha Bowman. I am an author, a professor, a business owner, a non-profit co-founder, a professional speaker, a mother, a wife, and a kind, compassionate, empathetic, yet imperfect person. And I'm crazy AF.

My dear friend, Elizabeth Lieba, recently wrote a book, *I'm Not Yelling: A Black Woman's Guide to Navigating the Workplace.*[37] The book tells her inspiring story of finding acceptance during her schooling years, whilst working in predominantly White spaces, and how she now walks her truth as a Black British child of Jamaican immigrants. In her book, she asks,

"Who are you? No, really. Who are you? Have you thought about who you are, how you feel, and you act when you are at your most comfortable and feel like your most authentic self? What does that look like to you?"

Those are some of the most thought-provoking questions you could ever ask yourself. Even if you are not in a marginalized group or never felt like you could not be your authentic self at work, imagine what it is like not feeling comfortable being yourself. That comes with a great privilege that we all should have. Research has demonstrated that when we work in authentic workspaces, we outperform others that do not. So, the case in point is, being authentic at work is paramount to our success, our happiness, and our motivation.

---

[37] Elizabeth Lieba, I'm Not Yelling: A Black Woman's Guide to Navigating the Workplace, Mango, December 13, 2022.

My friend, Anthony Paradiso, shared with me his journey of being a gay, cisgender man in the workplace. He didn't always feel comfortable being authentic at work which impacted his mental health tremendously. However, when he came out at work, a huge weight was lifted off of his shoulders. After coming out, his career eventually fell into place. He told me that "the sky's the limit, when one is able to freely be who they truly are, without judgment."

Now that you understand the connection between authenticity and mental well-being, let's circle back to the questions asked in Elizabeth Lieba's book. I challenge you to spend some quiet time reflecting on these plus a few more questions.

☐ Have you thought about who you are, how you feel, and act when you are at your most comfortable and feel like your most authentic self?

☐ What does that look like to you?

☐ Who or what is holding you back from being authentically you?

I have a short answer to that last question. The answer is YOU. You are holding yourself back from being authentically you.

Your time is limited, so don't waste it living someone else's life. Don't be trapped by dogma, which is living with the results of other people's thinking. Don't let the noise of others' opinions drown out your inner voice. And most important, have the courage to follow your heart and intuition. They somehow already know what you truly want to become. Everything else is secondary. - Steve Jobs

I agree with Jobs' truth so much. Our time is too limited to be trapped by other people's expectations and for our inner voices to be drowned by others' opinions. I am no longer concerned with how my outer appearance is perceived by others, how my accent sounds, or even if my living loudly with a mental illness ruffles a few feathers. I am more concerned with living each day to the fullest, giving myself space to reach my highest potential and to make mistakes. I want to extend that permission to you as well. Fill up spaces where you are accepted as who you are and support who you want to be. Keep in mind, you want to be celebrated, not tolerated. Where you are not considered brave to be fearlessly, authentically you.

Now that you've discovered or rediscovered who you are and where your passion lies, it's time for the next step in your journey.

Lean Into Transformation

Leaning into transformation may seem counterintuitive to leaning into acceptance of who you are. Nothing could be further from the truth. Once we accept who we are and are willing to show up at our workplaces authentically, we begin a transformation process. This transformation is magical. When we step into the workplace feeling confident, proud, and true to who we are, it can be incredibly empowering. Not only does our authenticity allow us to bring our most valuable skills and talents to the table, but it also encourages an open and honest dialogue with co-workers that strengthens relationships. When we can be open and honest, we are more likely to collaborate and create innovative solutions. Furthermore, when individuals feel accepted for who they are, it fosters a sense of belonging that can ripple through the entire organization—boosting morale, productivity, and overall satisfaction with the job and themselves.

When I was three years old, I entered my first beauty pageant. I don't remember this experience, but my mother told me that while the other contestants had to be literally dragged onto the stage by their mothers, I refused to let my mother accompany me. I climbed on that stage and did my own thing. I won that pageant and many more throughout my childhood. I did not win because I was the prettiest by any commercial beauty standards, but it was my confidence that won the judges over.

I carried most of that confidence into adulthood. Of course, there have been times when I have felt like an imposter, but for most of my career, I believed that I deserved to be in any room I entered. Early in life, I was fearlessly confident that I can achieve anything that I put my mind to and can overcome any obstacle in my way. Remember, I was tested on that second part when I faced open heart surgery at 11 years old. When I was diagnosed with bipolar disorder, it took some time, but I eventually became fearlessly confident that I would overcome certain negative outcomes that this condition could bring. After speaking to countless people facing challenges, I know I am not alone in thinking that being fearlessly confident is not easy by any means, but confidence is the next critical step to going from being burned out, unhappy, and unmotivated to reclaiming your mental health at work.

In the previous chapter, I shared how crucial it is that we can be both fearless and authentic at work. To unmask ourselves, however, we have to be confident in our abilities, opinions, knowledge, and skills. It is not that we do not possess these things, it is just that for so long, our credibility has been questioned. When dealing with the intricacies of the workplace, especially as it relates to challenges and pushing back on toxic work environments, our credibility will most likely be challenged. In Chapter 6, I wrote that in the workplace, it is not about *what* is right. It is about *who* is right.

Who does not make too much noise?
Who looks the part?
Who plays the part?
Who is bringing in the big bucks?
Who shares the same "values"?

Those traits seem to unfairly influence who gets heard, seen, and recognized. In other words, who has the most credibility? My husband asked me a challenging question the other day about why more people do not speak up about toxic people in the workplace and toxic work environments. A couple of years ago, I would have answered the question by saying that the number one reason that they do not speak up is due to the fear of retaliation. Today my perspective has changed. My answer now would be your lack of confidence that you would even be believed. Thinking back on my career, many people approached me with valid concerns about their work environment, but there were instances when I could not admit to them that they were right, their work environment sucked! I'm not saying that I was not working behind the scenes to remove the threats to their mental well-being, but some organizations just would not allow me to be honest and transparent in my role.

Eventually, that all changed. I had to rethink why these organizations were not letting me be transparent with their workforce about the shortcomings of their work environment. Were they truly not "letting me be transparent"? Why was I having to ask for permission? Part of my job as an HR leader was to identify opportunities for our organizations to be more inclusive, positive, and engaging. Those things were written in my job description, so why was I not doing that? Finally, I reached deep down into my soul to do what I had done when I was three years old: I rejected the hand-holding and micromanaging. I began to not let the constraints of my mind get the best of me and leaned into my confidence to do what was best for my organization and the employee. Those two things should not be mutually exclusive. This was a transformative experience.

Just like my early childhood experiences shaped my ability to show confidence in my abilities and influence in the workplace, the same can be true for those who have trouble finding their voice. Growing up, some of my elders would always say, "Be seen, not heard." That was always tough for me to listen to because I knew, even as a child, that being older does not necessarily mean you are wiser. It took everything in me to hold my tongue to correct the adults. Of course, there are other reasons why people have low confidence at work. Some of us have tried to speak up but were silenced for so long that we just gave up. So, as perfectly stated by Ann Howell, "low confidence is not an inherent flaw, and it doesn't have to define you. [...] It begins with becoming more self-aware, changing your mindset, and learning to bring your full self to work — or wherever you go."[38]

Building Confidence Begins with Self-Awareness

Self-awareness can significantly impact your confidence at work. When you are self-aware, you have a deep understanding of your strengths and weaknesses, your values, your emotions, and your thought patterns. This understanding can help you make better decisions, communicate more effectively, and manage your emotions more successfully.

Identifying your strengths and weaknesses is key to self-awareness. Just like I explained that there are people who are not confident sharing their expertise with their workplaces, I also know people who feel as if they always have to say something even when it is not meaningful or valuable. That last part is important to highlight because your overconfidence could be the cause of someone else's lack of confidence.

When you have a clear understanding of your strengths and weaknesses, you can focus on what you do best and improve areas where you may need to grow. This can help you feel more confident in your abilities and more prepared to take on new challenges. Other tips for building self-awareness include:

Understanding your values: When you know what is important to you, you can make decisions that align with your values. This can give you a sense of purpose and help you feel more confident in your choices.

Managing your emotions: When you are self-aware, you can better recognize and regulate your emotions. This can help you stay calm under pressure, communicate more effectively, and navigate challenging situations with greater ease.

---

[38] Ann Howell, How To Build Confidence at Work, Harvard Business Review, August 9, 2021, https://hbr.org/2021/08/how-to-build-confidence-at-work.

Recognize your thought patterns. When self-aware, you can identify negative thought patterns and replace them with more positive and empowering ones. This can help you overcome self-doubt and build greater confidence in your abilities.

One person who has mastered these concepts is one of the people I most admire today, the incomparable Michele Meyer-Shipp[39]. Her story of going from being burned out (and likely unhappy and unmotivated) to reclaiming her mental health, passion, and purpose at work is an amazing journey that most would not have the courage to embark upon. As a Black woman, she was the first person in her family to attend graduate school, then law school, and was on her way to becoming a partner at her law firm. She then left the legal field to pursue a career in HR and DEI, as well as becoming the first woman of color to be named the Chief People and Culture Officer for Major League Baseball (MLB) in 2020. However, her tenure in that position was short-lived when her son called to her attention how worn-out she looked when she arrived home one day. Living through a global pandemic, a racial reckoning, and being a Black woman "worried about [her] own children [and] safety," made her feel completely "tapped out." A year later, she left her high-profile role at MLB and took a lower-paying job as the CEO of Dress for Success.

Michele came to understand that for her to recover from being burned out and to prevent it from happening again, she had to recognize "that it was time for her to use her skills, talents, and capabilities to help and support those who are most vulnerable in ways that better reflected her caring nature." She was scared though to step into something she'd never done before and "was

---

[39] Jennifer Liu, 'Mom, you look really exhausted': How this CEO get her dream job, and then burnt out on it, CNBC Make It, November 6, 2022, https://www.cnbc.com/2022/11/06/dress-for-success-ceo-michele-c-meyer-shipp-on-burnout-career-advice.html#:~:text=The%20reality%20was%20that%20the,felt%20the%20same%20relentless%20exhaustion.

afraid [she] might let [her] family down." Even so, she says that she "never looked back." For her, "your best-made plans for your career may not be your endgame."[40] Doesn't that sound crazy and fearless? Michele's transformation from the person she thought she should be to the person she was meant to be, convinced me that what I have provided you in this book is not just guidance. It is a reality. We can all lean into our transformational journey toward mental well-being. We just need empowerment and confidence to begin our journey.

---

[40] Ibid.

CHAPTER 13

FEARLESSLY, NOT OKAY

Repeat after me.

 I'm not okay. I'm not okay. I'm not okay.

I am all for saying positive affirmations daily, and my husband and I often have to remind ourselves and each other, and our kids about all the positive things surrounding us. But sometimes the chemicals in our brains get disrupted, and we are not okay, despite our circumstances. Whether you have been diagnosed with a mental health condition like me or not, there will be times when you are not okay, and you need to say or do something about it. And I want to permit you to speak or take action. Before I was diagnosed with bipolar disorder, I think I should have been diagnosed with toxic positivity. Samara Quintero, LMFT, CHT, and Jamie Long, PsyD, define toxic positivity as "the excessive and ineffective overgeneralization of a happy, optimistic state across all situations."[41] Growing up and all the way into adulthood,

---

[41] Samara Quintero LMFT, CHT and Jamie Long PsyD, Toxic Positivity: The Dark Side of Positive Vibes, The Psychology Group, https://thepsychologygroup.com/toxic-

I was taught to always be grateful for there were others who had it worse than I did. So, whenever my brain started to send me signals that I wasn't okay, I would dismiss those signals and think, "someone out there is going through something worse." I would quickly invalidate my emotions and always look at the brighter side of things. At times, this positive outlook resulted in me dismissing valid feelings and emotions and caused me to let others cross those psychological boundaries which eventually resulted in harm. The process of toxic positivity results in the denial, minimization, and invalidation of the authentic human emotional experience. Essentially, you positively hide your pain and encourage others to do the same. Quintero and Long credit Brené Brown for suggesting that we often do this due to the shame of not being okay.

Remember my story of going through a bipolar disorder manic depressive episode during the early months of the COVID-19 pandemic even though my business had picked up and I had not yet experienced grief, job loss, or isolation like many others were experiencing? I felt so much shame that I was unhappy when I had so much to be grateful for. This shame eventually led to a suicide attempt and a long recovery. What would happen if we could shed shame and instead become fearlessly not okay? I know that my story could have taken a different direction, and so could the stories I shared with you in this book.

Everyone's story is different. Some fear asking for help due to shame or stigma. Others fear asking due to their religious beliefs. Some fear because they do not want to know the answer. Remember, there is such a thing as self-stigmatization, which causes many people not to want to know or accept their mental health condition. Whatever the case may be, I urge you to shed

---

positivity/#:~:text=What%20is%20Toxic%20Positivity%3F,the%20authenti c%20human%20emotional%20experience.

the fear and break the stigma of struggling with your mental health for yourself and others.

As we conclude this final chapter, I would like to leave you with some additional resources I have curated for when you're not okay.

Need More or Different Therapy Than What Your Company Provides? Check Out These Resources

Service/Organization	Description	Website
BetterUp	Matches individuals with career coaches to tap into your strengths so you can flourish at work.	betterup.com
Psych Central	Provides users with an array of mental health providers in their area.	https://psychcentral.com/
Psychology Today	Directory of therapist and treatment centers across the United States.	https://www.psychologytoday.com/us
National Alliance Mental Illness (NAMI)	Provides support groups and a helpline for various demographics.	https://nami.org/Home

Therapy for Black Girls	An online community dedicated to encouraging mental wellness for Black women and Black girls. *Therapy for Black Girls* also offers a referral tool to help users find mental health services.	https://therapyforblackgirls.com/
Black Men Heal	Provides mental health treatment, psycho-education, and support services to men of color. By providing free access to mental health services, *Black Men Heal* encourages Black men to share experiences of stigma, racial bias, and mental	https://blackmenheal.org/

	health issues with other Black men to help create safe spaces.	
Pride Counseling	Professional therapy for the LGBT community.	www.pridecounseling.com

Resources for Employers
Workplace Mental Health Training for Managers, HR, and Individual Contributors

Service/Organization	Description	Website
The Natasha Bowman Consulting Group	Provides strategic workplace mental well-being consulting and training.	natashabowman.com
Your Healthy Reality	Helps professionals gain self-awareness, become emotionally intelligent, and retrain their minds back on the path of positivity, which is the foundation to ensuring the whole person shows up to work.	https://www.yourhealthyreality.com/
Mentera	Mentera is the only community committed to creating connections between employers, payers, providers, and everyone in	https://joinmentera.com/

	between who is focused on mental health. I am honored to be a Global Ambassador for this organization.	
Nivati	Provides more than meditation and more than just counseling. *Nivati* includes many tools so every employee can get the support they need.	https://www.nivati.com/

CHAPTER 14

THE MENTAL HEALTH CONTINUUM

You've finally reached the last chapter of this book! I know that this book has taken you on an emotional roller coaster. Mental health is not the most delightful topic to discuss, but somebody had to do it. I'm so glad you have allowed me to share my stories, your stories, and insights about a topic that I am so passionate about, and I know many of you are too. As we come to a close, I want to leave you with one final thought regarding your mental health. I know I wrote about this previously, but treating your mental health as meticulously as we treat our physical health and outward appearance is vital. When I think about mental health, I think of it as being on a continuum, as in **"something that keeps on going and changing slowly over time**, like the continuum of the four seasons."[42] Think about that definition for a minute. Across the globe, we are experiencing different seasons. As I write this book, there is snow outside my window, while at the same time, it is considered summertime in Sydney, Australia. Other places are enjoying Spring. So, in most places, people experience every season throughout the year. When it comes to your mental health, what season are you in? Just like the four meteorological

---

[42] www.dictionary.com

seasons, I believe that your mental health journey is on a continuum of prevention, treatment, healing, and maintenance.

Mental Health Continuum

Prevention	Treatment	Healing	Maintenance
Take measures to prevent harm, triggers, trauma, and other variables from disrupting mental well-being.	Seek treatment to address and prevent harm, triggers, and other variables that have been identified that may disrupt your mental well-being.	Heal from grief, trauma, broken relationships, rejection, abandonment, and negative workplace experiences.	Maintain mental wellness by taking measures to prevent stressors to your mental health, seek proactive and reactive treatment, and heal from previous trauma and harm.

Knowing where you are in the Mental Health Continuum at any time allows you to take charge of your mental health.

 ## Prevention

Our ultimate goal is to prevent harm, triggers, trauma, and other variables from disrupting our mental well-being. I hope this book has provided plenty of insights into identifying and implementing intervention methods for these disruptors. Think about it. We all have daily routines that we engage in to prevent things from happening to our bodies. We do not want bad breath, cavities, or gum disease, so we brush our teeth daily. We take showers for cleanliness and to prevent body odor. Many of us take daily vitamins to supplement our food to prevent nutrient deficiencies. We do these things without even thinking about them and would be horrified if we somehow forgot to do some of these things. My question to you is, what daily preventative measures are you taking to promote your mental well-being? We discussed many preventative measures throughout this book, but here's a reminder. I challenge you to add your own to this list.

Eliminate Toxicity

- **Choose Your Thoughts Wisely:** Recognize when you are engaging in toxic thoughts and take action to stop them. Replace negative thoughts with a positive outlook. Additionally, distance yourself from toxic people. If someone brings negativity to your life, consider limiting or eliminating your contact with them. If that person happens to be in your workplace, I have already provided you with a strategy for exiting that harm.
- **Practice Mindfulness:** Take a few moments each day to be mindful of your thoughts and feelings. This can help you become more aware of what is happening in your life and how it affects you.

Connect with Others

- Make an effort to stay connected with family, friends, and other supportive people in your life.

Manage Stress

- Develop healthy coping strategies to help you manage stress, so it does not affect your mental health.

Treatment

Adding to the factors included in the prevention part of the continuum, you should develop a relationship with a mental health provider even if you have not experienced or are currently not experiencing a mental health crisis. I don't know about you, but I love when I walk into a doctor's office and feel a certain level of familiarity and comfort. This is true even if I am just going in for an annual physical exam. It is also insightful when the doctors can review my charts and inform me about any positive progress I have made with my blood work and weight management or if there are areas that I need improvement to live a long, healthy life. Before my bipolar disorder diagnosis, I did not have that kind of relationship with a mental health provider. Let me tell you, it took a lot of energy, emotion, and sometimes embarrassment to divulge every aspect of my life for the past forty-plus years. I am sure there were some things I did not even remember that would have been relevant to my situation. And let's not forget some of the horror stories I experienced while searching for a provider I could finally trust and connect with. I can only imagine my experience had I been proactive in developing a relationship with a mental health provider before my diagnosis. Would I have been diagnosed sooner? Would my manic episodes have been prevented? Would there have been an intervention in my suicide attempt? At this point, I can only hypothesize. What I know for sure is that there would not have been any downside to my seeking treatment sooner.

Healing

At some point in our lives, we will need healing. We must heal from grief, trauma, broken relationships, rejection, abandonment, and, yes, even from our experiences at work. Healing is crucial to protecting our mental health. It is also part of the prevention and treatment parts of the continuum. If we do not heal from past experiences that have negatively impacted our mental health, preventing other harmful things from affecting us is difficult. To heal, oftentimes, we need treatment. Unresolved trauma from life experiences can show up in many forms that impact us and those around us. If we have not healed from unresolved trauma, managing our emotions, such as anger, fear, resentment, and sadness, can become difficult.

I shared with you earlier in this book that my bipolar manic episode resulted in reckless behavior and damage to my family. Again, I'm not ready to share all the details yet, but the episode caused much collateral damage, especially to my loving husband. After I was diagnosed, we both focused on my treatment and healing but failed to focus on his. It has taken us years to realize how much healing he needed and how not focusing on his healing impacted his mental health.

 ## Maintenance

Last but not least in the mental health continuum is maintaining your mental well-being. Assuming that you have been following the mental health continuum by taking preventive actions, seeking treatment, and healing from past trauma, you should also work to maintain your mental well-being. The only way to do this is to follow the mental health continuum unceasingly. Although I use the word journey from time to time regarding mental health, that is not what it is. A journey assumes that there is a destination. Technically, there is, and that destination is that you reach a positive, healthy state of mind. However, life happens. And you need to be prepared for the inevitable challenges you will likely face. However, by following the continuum, you will learn to be more resilient when facing those challenges. I am not suggesting excessive resilience, but you will be more mentally prepared.

I often hear people say, "Check on your strong friends." I hate that statement. What does it mean to be strong? Am I strong because I do not outwardly express emotions? Am I strong because I appear to be resilient? Am I strong because I appear to be successful and accomplished? Maybe those things define being strong, but I want to add to these sentiments. I think the strongest people in the world are willing to admit they need help. They are willing to say, "I'm carrying too much weight on my back." Or "I need a shoulder to cry on." Or "I need to step away to take care of my mental health." In workplaces around the globe, there is an expectation of the "excessive resilience" I spoke about earlier.

Excessive resilience in the workplace can be a detrimental factor to employees' morale. The pressure to maintain resilience when faced with the same organizational challenges over and over again can lead to burnout and fatigue. To reclaim your mental health in the workplace, you must be willing to take risks, accept that your mental health and wealth are not mutually exclusive, and enter into the mental health continuum at whichever season you are in your life. As we come to the end of this book, I leave you with a question posed by my cousin and fitness and wellness expert, Pamela Bartee,

"Are you a human being or a human doing?"

That question made me pause to reflect. When I reflect on this question as it relates to how we work, oftentimes, we are just humans doing. We are doing what is expected of us and frequently beyond what is expected, but we expect little in return besides our paychecks. Let's shift from "human doing" to "human being." Let's be humans who are intentional in how, where, and to whom we lend our talents. Notice I used the word lend. Our workplaces do not own our talents. They are simply borrowing them. If you let someone borrow something from you, you typically ask that it is returned to you in good condition. When we lend ourselves to our organizations, the expectation should be that our organizations do not misuse or abuse us. We expect that when we separate from our organizations and our "lending" period is over, we will be in good or better condition than when we entered. Is that too much to ask? I do not believe so.

*****

It's been over two years since I was diagnosed with bipolar disorder. Since then, I've spent countless hours evaluating my life, mainly in the workplace. I've often asked myself, "If I got a do-over, would I spend so much time at work?" Surprisingly, my answer has consistently been "Yes." Lots of people look forward to retirement, but not me. I've loved my work, especially when I could do it in a safe, positive, and healthy workplace.

Whether I've worked as an HR executive in a Fortune 500 company or a healthcare organization or served in a more boutique capacity as a consultant, my work has brought me a profound sense of purpose. I've made a difference.

Everyone is looking to thrive at work. I believe organizations don't intend to avoid getting between employees and their flourishing. But when business becomes *busy*ness, leaders lose focus on their people and what will help them excel. They want more and more fruit—profit, prestige, power—but neglect the roots from which these ambitions grow. In other words, to increase profit and productivity, leaders must focus on the root, not the fruit. Long hours, exclusion, isolation, toxicity, and a hundred other micro-assaults against their employees' mental health choke those roots and blight whatever fruit comes from them. Employees suffer, companies struggle, and everyone wonders what's gone wrong.

Let's examine the soil representing our workplace culture and ask a few hard questions. Are we creating an environment where *everyone* can flourish? Are we tending to our employees' psychological, social, spiritual, and physical needs? Or, are we ignoring the roots and misusing synthetic fertilizer (bonuses, perks, programs, etc.), which over time harms the environment by depleting the soil of nitrogen, oxygen, and critical bacteria that ultimately produce healthy plants? Synthetic fertilizers such as bonuses and perks will provide a momentary flourish rather than lasting growth. For the good of our companies and employees, we need to quit settling for superficial quick fixes and focus on the root causes of our disfunctions. When we do that, we'll create workplaces where *all* our employees—regardless of mental ability or disability—can gladly spend their lives doing work that bears good fruit. Employees will not only work for profit, but they will also work with purpose - they will work for something bigger which will positively impact their mental health and the health and success of the organization.

As I mentioned earlier, I was labeled and often used the moniker of the Workplace Doctor. As the Workplace Doctor, I offer you to select between two prescriptions. In so, I will paraphrase the character Morpheus from the first Matrix movie. "If you take the blue pill, you will continue to create and work in psychologically dangerous work environments. If you take the red pill, you and your organization will thrive with purpose and achieve unimaginable success. Which pill will you take?

ACKNOWLEDGEMENTS

It's amazing what happens when life throws you a curve ball. I never imagined in a million years that I would be writing a book about my experience with being diagnosed with bipolar disorder and becoming a global mental health advocate. However, I am grateful for the many friends, family, clients, and platforms that have allowed me to share my story to reduce the stigma of mental illness.

Before I wrote this book, I was offered publishing deals from major publishing houses to use their platform to share my story. I declined their offers. I wanted to use this opportunity to have complete creative control of this project and to extend opportunities to others whose talents and creativity are often overlooked. Those people include people with mental health conditions who are judged by their conditions and not by the value they offer. As such, I carefully curated a wealth of talent from diverse backgrounds to assist me with completing this project. If you have a project to which these exceptional, talented people can lend their expertise, please give them an opportunity.

Book Cover Design: Jane Rade
Book Cover Photo of Natasha Bowman: Nick F. Nelson
Book Formatting: Hyacinth Oyekezie
Book Editors: Annetta Benzar
　　　　　　　Jill Mckellan
　　　　　　　Kenny Silva
Graphic Design: Joy Murphy
Logo Design: Unbong Koffi
Research: Leah Williams

I would be remiss if I didn't give a special acknowledgment to my wonderful, supportive husband, Kent. When we said our vows of "in sickness and health," he had no idea that sickness would include mental illness. However, your support, partnership, and commitment have been unwavering. For that, I am forever grateful.

If this book has inspired you to join the movement of breaking the stigma of mental illness in the workplace and beyond, please take a moment to donate to our non-profit, The Bowman Foundation for Workplace Equity and Mental Wellness, at . Some of the proceeds from the sales of this book will go to funding our mission. However, funding is a fundamental part of us sustaining our efforts.

The Natasha Bowman Consulting Group (NBCG), formerly Performance ReNEW, is a pioneering consulting firm that fosters mental wellness and psychological safety in the workplace. Our mission is to help organizations cultivate thriving, healthy, and engaging environments where employees can unlock their full potential and contribute meaningfully to their teams.

We offer comprehensive, end-to-end strategic solutions designed to create positive and supportive work cultures. Our data-driven approach is tailored to each organization's unique needs, ensuring our clients receive the best possible outcomes. Our services include:

Cultural Assessments: We evaluate the current state of an organization's work culture, identifying areas of strength and opportunities for improvement to form the foundation for targeted interventions.

Training Programs: Our custom-designed training programs provide employees with the knowledge and skills to promote mental wellness and psychological safety within their teams. These programs cover emotional intelligence, workplace mental health training for managers, HR, and individuals, resilience, psychological safety, and mindfulness.

Leadership Development: We work closely with leaders at all levels to enhance their understanding of mental health and psychological safety and to develop their capacity to foster supportive work environments. Our workshops and coaching sessions help leaders embody and promote the principles of mental wellness throughout their organizations.

Strategic Development: We partner with clients to create and implement actionable strategies to transform workplace culture. We support organizations in developing policies, processes, and systems that prioritize employee well-being and engagement.

To find out more on how your organization can benefit from a partnership with The Natasha Bowman Consulting group or to book Natasha Bowman as a keynote speaker at your next event, visit:

NATASHABOWMAN.COM

MEET THE AUTHOR
NATASHA BOWMAN, JD

Recognized as a LinkedIn Top Voice for Workplace Mental Health, a Top 30 Global Guru for Management, and Top 200 Voices in leadership, Natasha Bowman, JD, SPHR has labored to transform the American workplace from the inside out for nearly 20 years. As a champion for employees, she's worked with a broad range of organizations as a c-suite HR executive to create an engaging environment in which employees are respected, genuine leaders are cultivated, and top performance is achieved. Natasha is an award-winning, modern-day pioneer of workplace equality, inspiring organizations to not just pay lip service to workplace rights but craft highly-engaged cultures where *every* employee is truly dignified and valued for their contribution. Because of her ability to diagnose workplace issues and provide proven solutions to organizations, she is often referred to as The Workplace Doctor.

Natasha Bowman has developed a reputation as an expert workplace consultant through her firm, The Natasha Bowman Consulting Group, formerly known as, Performance ReNEW and as a labor and employment law attorney. Her clients include 4A's, Forbes, Hearst Magazines, Google, Trip Adviser, Microsoft, and R/GA, to name a few. Apart from her rich expertise and cross-sector experience, she brings an ardent intellectual commitment to the field by serving as an adjunct professor of human resources for distinguished institutions such as Georgetown University, Fordham University, Manhattan College, and The Jack Welch Management Institute.

She is a sought after TedX and international keynote speaker for conferences and organizations worldwide and has shared her passion for creating positive and engaging workplaces by speaking across the globe for organizations and events such as The HR Congress in Nice, France, New York Police Department, The City of Detroit, Ford Motor Company, The Employers' Association, Temple University, Harvard University, Toledo Public Schools, Microsoft, and the Society for Human Resources Management. Her expertise is frequently quoted in national publications such as Forbes, Business Insider, Cosmopolitan Magazine, U.S. News and World Reports, The Wall Street Journal and the LA Times.

She is a three-time best-selling published author and the co-founder of The Bowman Foundation for Workplace Equity and Mental Wellness. Her anticipated third book CRAZY AF: How to go from being burned out, unmotivated & unhappy to reclaiming your mental health at work was published in 2023.